SilverSmith

SILVERSMITH

A Biography of Walter Smith

❖

Neil Drysdale

BIRLINN

First published in 2007 by
Birlinn Limited
West Newington House
10 Newington Road
Edinburgh
EH9 1QS

www.birlinn.co.uk

ISBN 13: 978 1 84158 629 8
ISBN 10: 1 84158 629 3

British Library Cataloguing-in-Publication Data
A catalogue record for this book is available from the British Library

Designed and typeset by Iolaire Typesetting, Newtonmore
Printed and bound by CPI Mackays, Chatham, Kent

CONTENTS

❖

ACKNOWLEDGEMENTS

❖

I would like to thank Craig Brown, Terry Butcher, Ewan Camp-
bell, Ronnie Esplin, Andy Goram, Jim Guy, Sandy Jardine, Ally
McCoist, Robert McElroy, Scott Nisbet, Alan Rough, Stephen
Smith, Colin Stein, Sandy Tyrie, the Scottish Football Museum
and Chick Young. Thanks are also in order to a number of former
Rangers players and supporters, who asked for their contributions to remain anonymous, although since the majority of these
respondents were expressing praise for Walter Smith, this shyness
was sometimes difficult to understand.

I would also like to thank Neville Moir at Birlinn for his
patience during what was a difficult summer, and my agent,
Mark Stanton, for exuding his usual calmness under pressure.
Duggie Middleton worked assiduously in editing the original
manuscript with his usual diligence. Finally, my wife, Dianne,
had to tolerate me deploying my thumping two-finger typing
style, often until 4.30 in the morning, and remained a pillar of
support throughout the project, for which I thank her.

Neil Drysdale

CHAPTER ONE

A MAN IN THE CROWD

❖

'This club is different. This is Rangers Football Club'

Long before there came Heysel or Hillsborough with their relent-lessly grim television images, incongruous floral tributes and uncomprehending vales of tears, there was one Saturday evening in Glasgow on which mothers and fathers, sons and daughters and many friends of friends clung anxiously to the hope that their loved ones would eventually make it home, and confirm that they had escaped the Ibrox Disaster. The majority did come home, and others such as Walter Smith, Alex Ferguson and Andy Roxburgh clambered around the mangled heaps of bodies and stricken souls, the emergency workers and Old Firm volunteers on Stair-way 13, and thanked their lucky stars before absorbing the enormity of what had transpired. For 66 other families there was the spectre of a long night's journey into the void, and recognition that the catastrophe which engulfed Ibrox stadium at the end of the New Year match on 2 January 1971, had snatched away their menfolk, and in Margaret Ferguson's case, her daughter.

Decades on, pictures from the newsreels reflect collective mys-tification and bewilderment, accompanied by a sense of futile anger at the casual fashion in which so many lives were sacrificed. But beyond that is a numbness among the grieving families, possibly reflecting their feeling that such hackneyed phrases as

1

'Time is a great healer' and 'They're in a better place now' are but platitudes for those fortunate enough never to have been obliged to identify relatives with faces blackened and life squeezed out of them. Talk to men such as Smith, Sandy Jardine or John Greig – hard-nosed artisans from an industrial background – and you will not hear easy sentiments, but rather hushed voices and instinctive sympathy for victims who, in other circumstances, could have been their very selves. Then prod them gently on their memories of that ghastly event, and they will relate their accounts of a tragedy which, all too fleetingly, tore through Glasgow's sectarian curtain and saw Orangemen shed tears in the company of priests throughout the west of Scotland and yonder into Edinburgh, before snaking across the Forth Bridge to the Kingdom of Fife and the community of Markinch, where Peter Easton, Richard Morrison, David Patton, Mason Phillips and Bryan Todd, schoolboys who lived within a few hundred yards, perished together on that stairway, which had witnessed an accident in 1961 and near-disasters in 1967 and '69.

Sandy Jardine, one of the celebrated ex-players who still walks the corridors of Rangers FC, describes the terrible events:

'In these days, this was probably the biggest fixture of the season, considering that the Old Firm clubs only met twice a year, but it was dreadfully ironic that what had been a fairly good-natured occasion, with neither trouble on the terraces nor on the pitch, should develop into a waking nightmare for so many people. Everybody knows the circumstances whereby Jimmy Johnstone sent Celtic in front with a minute to go. The ball got centred, we equalised at once [through Colin Stein] and the referee blew full-time immediately. So you had Rangers supporters who thought: "Oh, that's the game over" when Jimmy scored turning to go down the big staircase, then turning back when they heard the huge roar which greeted Colin's strike, and that coincided with a massive number of spectators making their path towards the exit and the subway. Then suddenly somebody fell, and the whole terrible business began.

'The thing is that I was on the ground staff, I had actually swept these stairways, and they were huge, really solid objects, so I could never understand how they could get mangled so badly by any number of human beings. But they were. Just think of it: the pressure of all those bodies cascading over one another and the panic which must have spread . . . Ach, there are no words in the dictionary to describe adequately what happened during those next few minutes. But you have to realise that we as players were completely unaware anything was wrong at that stage. We were in the dressing room fairly happy to have managed a draw, just sharing a few laughs together before getting into the bath. Well, I was one of the last guys to climb out, but as I re-emerged the order came that there had been an accident, and we all had to leave the room as quickly as possible. It could have been a fire alert or anything, but while we started putting our clothes on as fast as we could, the authorities started to bring some of the dead bodies into the place, and as you can probably imagine, everybody turned grey at the sight of them. But even then we had no real idea of the extent of the fatalities.

'As I drove back to my home in the east end of Edinburgh, I heard there were two dead, but soon enough the figures mounted up. It was 12, then 22, then 30, then 44 – I don't know why, but that number sticks in my mind – and finally it climbed to 66 as the news filtered out to all the parents and kith and kin of the folk who had attended the match, and then gone to pubs or restaurants or picture-houses afterwards. I have spoken to hundreds of fans since 1971, and they have told me of how vast crowds assembled at all of the drop-off points for the buses to find out whether their loved ones were okay. The telephone lines were jammed, Glasgow was in turmoil, the hospitals were all packed to overflowing. Anxiety, terror, pain, sadness, horror . . . a blanket of all these emotions was draped over the whole country that night, but there was nothing remotely comforting about it.'

Amid this hellish vista, Willie Waddell, the Rangers manager, somehow offered a semblance of sanity. It was significant that he and Celtic counterpart Jock Stein had observed casualties in other spheres, whether in battle or at the coal-face, and the pair constantly emphasised the desperate need for entrenched communities to pull together, and for religious tribalism to be cast aside. Sadly, but perhaps inevitably given the illogical nature of the positions adopted by extremists on both sides, the so-called healing process proved little more than a nine-day wonder. Yet in the longer term, the calamity yielded some benefits. Waddell, for example, vowed that the scenes he had witnessed would never be repeated at Ibrox, and before his death in 1992 that objective had borne fruit in the creation of a magnificent new stadium. Not that anybody connected with 1971 would forget the condition of the old edifice. 'It's strange what comes into your mind, but when I first went to the top of the steps and gazed down on the pile of bodies, my initial thought was of Belsen, because the corpses were entangled as they had been in the pictures which came out of the concentration camps,' Waddell told *The Scotsman* newspaper's illustrious football correspondent John Rafferty. 'But my God, it was dreadful: there were bodies in the dressing rooms, in the gymnasium and even in the laundry room. My own training staff and the Celtic boys were working flat out at the job of resuscitation, and we were all trying everything possible to bring breath back to those crushed limbs. Honestly, I will never forget the sight of Bob Rooney, the Celtic physiotherapist, with tears in his eyes giving the kiss of life to innumerable victims. He never stopped, nor did the Rangers doctors, nor the nurses and ambulance staff who flocked to join them, and we will never know how many lives were saved in there in that frenzy of activity.'

Nearby, the Southern General Hospital was under siege, their switchboard of only 35 lines, plus a single police short-wave radio, jammed by a crescendo of panic-stricken calls. But by midnight a worse task was in prospect for the likes of Jardine, Waddell, Greig and Colin Stein, who seems troubled to this day by the notion that his goal might have been a catalyst for such carnage: the funerals. And the subsequent protracted search for answers allied to the quest for apportioning responsibility which, despite lengthy inquiries, discovered little beyond the tinder-box of ingredients that would also bring death and destruction to the environs of Heysel and to Bradford and Hillsborough as much as 18 years later.

❖

Inside Ibrox, one fellow had stood intently throughout that Old Firm encounter transfixed by proceedings that were typically pulsating and frenetic. As a registered professional player with Dundee United, Walter Smith would not have been anywhere near Glasgow, let alone Govan, but for his acceptance that he was not good enough to merit inclusion in the Tannadice side's festive plans, and was therefore free to travel to the ground he regarded as his spiritual home, the place where his grandfather had taken him to behold what old Jock had considered the best team in the world. At 22 years of age, Smith strode into Ibrox that afternoon with hardly a care. He was a phlegmatic individual, a young man of substance with a trade as an electrician already acquired, just in case football work proved to be in short supply, and even in those formative days he had started to appreciate that, irrespective of the fact that as a player he would never join the likes of Jim Baxter, Jimmy Johnstone and Billy McNeill in the Scottish Football Association's Hall of Fame, he might have a part to play for his country further down the line. Indeed, Smith's recollection of the Ibrox Disaster epitomises many of the core values that have shone through his ascent to the summit of soccer management:

'I can remember leaving the stadium with my brother at the finish of the match. I was on Dundee United's books at the time, but because of my lack of ability they had omitted to select me for the New Year match, so I travelled to Ibrox on the supporters' club bus, and I remember there being a wall at the side of the staircase which, if it hadn't been there, would have allowed people to spill over. Both of us got out, I thought because the fencing had collapsed, but on the 25th anniversary I looked at a photograph and the fencing was intact. We must have got over the top of other people, although nobody around us was in any danger; the deaths occurred at the bottom of the stairs, but we didn't know that at the time. We got on the bus, which didn't have a radio or anything, and it was only when I arrived home that I remember my mother crying, saying people had died. If we had left two minutes earlier, it would have been us.'

Histrionics are not in Smith's nature, and his composure in discussing the Ibrox Disaster originated from the lessons he had learned growing up in visceral communities, where emotions tended to be best kept in check. In the days after 2 January he absorbed the consequences of the calamity which had befallen so many Scots by diabolical chance, but unlike many young foot-ballers he did not stick his head in the sand or seek refuge in alcohol. Instead, Smith read about the tragic stories of those who had been killed, swiftly recognised that the extended Rangers family had been dealt a devastating blow and pledged that he would do what he could to heal the widespread hurt. At the time he was in no position to swoop to the rescue, but as the years unfolded he never forgot the fundamental experiences of 1971.

The voices of that awful evening still resonate among those who were there, as I discovered when tracking down some of the eye-witnesses. 'I always remember standing in the middle of Stairway 13 and looking at this pile of bodies, some of them black, some of them blue, lying like rag dolls on all sides of me, whilst other fans were desperately grappling on to whatever they could find to avoid falling into the carnage,' recalls Andrew Ewan, a head librarian in Dunoon, who was 23 in 1971. 'I was at the match on my own because my best mate was in Aberdeen with his parents, and with hindsight I believe that one of the reasons why I survived is that I was wearing slip-on shoes, and I lost them as hundreds of supporters were caught up in the crush. I know that might sound strange, but I'm convinced that if I had been wearing shoes with laces, as I normally did, I wouldn't have been able to wriggle out of the morass. But I was tall and skinny in these days, and somehow I escaped.

'Yet in retrospect it always occurs to me that any of us could have been killed, that this was an accident waiting to happen and that you could drive yourself mad trying to rationalise why some survived and others perished. By the time the emergency services reached the scene and started working their guts out to rescue as many of the injured as they could, I was in shock, and I remember a policeman approaching me and saying: "Go home, son. Go home to your loved ones. There's nothing you can do here." That was the helpless feeling which engulfed us all when we woke up the following morning. It brought us all together, Rangers and Celtic fans, united in a common grief. But sadly it didn't last long.'

Craig Smith, a Livingston-based glazier, was not present at Ibrox, but the escalation into tragedy still haunts him. 'My father George was heading off for the Old Firm match, and as he put his coat on I asked if I could go along with him. But he just laughed, and after pointing out that my two older brothers also weren't going with him because it was too big a game, he waved us all goodbye. Well, at about ten to five there was a news-flash on the TV reporting that there had been an accident at Ibrox, but the programme had no details of any injuries. My mother looked worried, and although she wasn't too concerned at the outset, she became increasingly anxious as the time passed, because she and my father had arranged to go to a golf club dance that night. The later it grew you could tell that something was terribly wrong by my mum's expression, and she was constantly on the phone. Then suddenly the doorbell rang. My brother Stephen went to answer it, my mum screamed, then Stephen and my other brother George were standing together with tears streaming down their cheeks, and for a few moments I couldn't understand what on earth was going on.

'Eventually, though, we learned the truth. That while my dad had managed to push his brother John and brother-in-law Alex over the fence, he himself had been swept away with the force of the crowd, and even as John shouted towards him, he saw him die, upright. The very life was squeezed out of him on that terrible, terrible afternoon. At the time we lived in house No. 66 on the 14th floor, although you had to walk down to the living room on the 13th floor. So my father was born on the 14th of August, was killed on the 13th stair, and was one of the 66 killed at Ibrox. I will never forget it.'

In many respects the 1970s still seem within touching distance, but in other ways they belong to a different world. In the distinctly remote possibility of a recurrence of the Ibrox Disaster, television coverage nowadays would be wall-to-wall, obliterating everything else on the schedules. As darkness descended on 2 January 1971, however, Walter Smith, professional footballer, and Craig Smith, pre-school child, were in the dark about the scale of the calamity unfolding at their favourite club. Retired TV executive Bill Malcolm recalls: 'At that time, in my role as the director of the Saturday night football programme *Sportsreel*, we were out of the loop once the Old Firm match finished, whereas when you fast-forward three decades you have Sky, News 24, CNN, Ceefax, the Internet, breaking stories delivered straight to your phone or your iPod . . . all manner of up-to-the-minute news technology. In 1971 we had the *Green Citizen* sports paper reporting that three supporters had died at Ibrox. And that was it.

'Afterwards, some of us at the BBC were criticised for not having pictures of the disaster, but you have to realise that news and sport were entirely separate entities at the time, and there was no blurring of distinctions. All the same, there was never any question of us going ahead with plans to screen highlights of the game, and let's face it, on that evening an awful lot of people decided they would never again describe somebody missing a penalty as a *tragedy*, because the match at Ibrox didn't matter at all in the grand scheme of things. Life couldn't continue as normal in these circumstances.

However, I was involved later in the fatal accident inquiry, and I remember the pressure which was put on my secretary to recall the exact moment when the disaster started. Obviously it was a very painful experience for everyone caught up in the search for answers, and the job of dishing out blame. But, of course, we got off lightly, didn't we? We were still alive to be able to discuss the minutiae of what should and shouldn't have been done on that Saturday. The grieving families had no such get-out.'

❖

From Walter Smith's perspective, nothing would ever be quite the same after the winter of 1971. Born in Lanark in 1948, he had grown up in industrial Glasgow during a period when the metropolis truly fulfilled its reputation as the second city of the British Empire, and he was habitually a man at ease with his roots. By turns introspective, proud and competitive, his demeanour deadpan, sometimes even dour, Smith and Rangers were inextricably linked through his family background and his temperament. Endlessly restive, unsympathetic towards those who indulged in complacency, but fiercely protective of those he considered his friends, even at the age of eight the young Walter would stand up to bullies and was unafraid of the gangs who battled for the ascendancy on their patches of turf across Glasgow in the 1960s and '70s. He quickly found himself drawn towards Rangers with their history, their reputation as giants within the British game, and their cussed refusal to become trendy. Why else, with the advent of the Swinging Sixties and Beatlemania and social revolution effecting a transformation in the ideas of young Scots, would Smith be so fascinated by the Calvinist tradition which permeated Ibrox? That he certainly was. But then it is difficult to picture this individual as anything other than middle-aged, with a tie-rack, trouser-press and Brylcreem, a noted concoction for grooming gentlemen's hair, as essential elements in his bedroom.

None of this should be seen as criticism. After all, if everyone appeared the height of fashion, life would be pretty tedious, but it must be said that Walter Smith was conventional. He played football before starting school in Carmyle, was inducted into the Rangers fraternity by his grandfather, and watched the 1953 team thrash Queen of the South 6-0 with the sort of wonder that many of his contemporaries reserved for the latest science-fiction film. And so began a passionate love affair with the game that has burned more brightly than anything in his existence. And that's it. Smith had three priorities etched in his mind: football, football and football, and his formative years were occupied in watching Rangers, reading about Rangers and discussing club stalwarts such as Eric Caldow and Jimmy Millar with the ubiquitous Jock, whose influence ensured that his grandson never forgot the importance of tradition. The word is central to Smith's philosophy, and can be brought up to date with his commitment to support the Union, an issue which manifested itself in 2007 prior to Holyrood parliamentary elections, when his name appeared in the company of a string of senior footballing figures, including Billy McNeill, Ally McCoist and Sir Alex Ferguson, urging that Scotland remain part of the United Kingdom. That said, Smith has not jumped on any passing political bandwagon. No, he has always believed implicitly in old-fashioned values, whether in sport or in life, but especially in his career at Ibrox, expressed thus:

'Every single thing that happens at the club is related to something that happened here before. There is always someone around the place who will remind you of that. Or there will be someone who says: "Old Bill [former manager Bill Struth] wouldn't have done that." Or: "Deedle [Willie Waddell] would have done it this way." And you listen to that. I know there are those people who say that you cannot operate on history or live in the past, but that is not a view I agree with. When you have a club with a rich tradition, then you examine that tradition and take from it what can still remain important to the club in any era. It's something which is almost tangible when you walk into the foyer at Ibrox, and you live with these feelings every day of your life, and you can learn from the club's history.

'We have always had the tradition at Ibrox, for example, that players have to report for training wearing a collar and tie, and despite recent objections to this, that's the way it will stay. Sure it's a little strange when you first arrive from another club to find that rule in place. But if you think about it, maybe that's why it was there in the first place: to remind each and every player that this is not just any club. This club is different. This is Rangers Football Club, and it works because the players *do* wear collar and tie, and they all understand why that is being done. To wit, that it is another small way in which the club was set apart from other clubs in Scotland when the traditions were first being born.'

Walter Smith can appear a relic of the Struth era or even a soccer-style Mr Pooter, being fastidious to a fault, quietly obsessed with detail and equipped with a boffin's brain for arcane rules and regulations. Yet it is an injustice to portray him as a stuffed shirt. Down the years I have heard a litany of criticisms of Smith, the majority centring on the allegation that he has been a lucky manager who was in the right place at the right time, namely close to David Murray's well-stuffed wallet when Celtic seemed to pursue ever-ascending levels of debt and mediocrity. While there may be a modicum of truth in such complaints, the charges ultimately fail to reflect reality on three counts. Firstly, because Smith was well respected from his managerial exertions at Dundee United before he arrived at Ibrox in 1986. Secondly, because no football club, regardless of the chairman's wealth, can dominate a national championship by winning nine successive titles, as did Rangers from 1989–97, without being blessed with talented direction. And thirdly, because after Berti Vogts' unfortunate spell as Scotland's manager, most of the men who had floundered within his regime performed well for Smith. Are we saying that the man was fortunate once again, that in the few months between Vogts' troops stumbling to ignominy in Moldova and Smith's personnel orchestrating victory over France, a glorious new crop of national heroes emerged? Of course not! For the most part, Smith had to work with the modest resources that had been available to his unfortunate predecessor, and the difference was that the Scot brought purpose, commitment and tactical nous to the international campaign. He deserves credit for his achievements.

❖

Early in his first managerial spell at Rangers, when he co-operated with Graeme Souness, Smith reflected that walking through the Ibrox corridors and inspecting the committee rooms was akin to visiting a museum. Everything was pristine, photographs on the walls were lovingly mounted, and staff from boot room bombardiers to club newspaper employees constantly sported glints in their eyes, as if they had reached the zenith of their ambitions. For some that was probably true, but what was sufficient for the boys of the old brigade was not enough for Smith, despite his devotion to tradition, and certainly not for the ambitious Souness. If they had to implement unpopular decisions and risk offending some sensitivities at Ibrox, so be it. Both recognised that popularity contests have no place in football, especially considering the slough of despond into which Rangers had plummeted during the decade before they took over. Hence the necessity of clearing away the cobwebs and effecting a transformation of an increasingly moribund institution into a streamlined organisation that was fit for modern times. Souness has been accorded most of the praise for persuading a string of England internationalists, including Terry Butcher, Chris Woods and Graham Roberts, to travel to Glasgow to join the Rangers metamorphosis. So too he has garnered accolades for his reputedly brave stance in signing Roman Catholic striker Maurice 'Mo' Johnston from under

Celtic's noses in 1989. Nonetheless, the notion that the former Liverpool player was single-handedly responsible for tearing down decades-old barriers of prejudice does not stand up to scrutiny. On the contrary, while Souness was the public face of the Murray-driven bandwagon, excoriating rival players and pressmen alike, whether it be Hibernian's George McCluskey or *Glasgow Herald* journalist James Traynor, and fulfilling his role as hatchet-man of the Thatcher generation, it was Smith who toiled quietly and relentlessly behind the scenes, displaying some of the essential attributes that have made him so admired by Sir Alex Ferguson. In essence, Souness contributed ample sound and fury while Smith supplied the substance, and the divergent paths in their careers since the former departed Ibrox emphasise how his sharp suits and immaculate grooming were no match for his colleague's off-the-peg wisdom.

Indeed, it can be argued that Souness's role in elevating the expectation levels has had potentially ruinous consequences for those who have followed in his wake. Smith continued to be the beneficiary of his chairman's largesse beyond the mid-1990s, but by that stage it had become increasingly difficult to entice European-class talents to Scotland, particularly once the English premiership structure roared over the horizon. Celtic aficionados can respond with the name of Henrik Larsson, and I would add another couple of characters to accompany the exalted Swede: Lubomir Moravcik and Michael Mols. But the truth is that despite the acquisition of a past-his-peak Paul Gascoigne and a ridiculously over-priced Tore Andre Flo, Smith's stewardship owed more to the virtues of the River Clyde than to the Danube. Quite simply, he was placed in a situation which demanded all his powers of resilience, tenacity and fine-tuning, not least once the crafty Fergus McCann defied the rules of football business by staying true to his word and resuscitating the Celtic cause.

Any fair-minded analysis of Smith's career needs to acknowledge the failures on his CV. When he exited Ibrox and signed up with Everton in 1998, some acolytes initially insisted that he could emulate the success achieved by Ferguson, a fellow Glaswegian, at Manchester United. As the months passed and the Goodison Park odyssey developed into a trying adventure for Smith, some of these optimists sought to rewrite history with the declaration that the Merseyside club had made promises to the manager which were not delivered. However, having spoken to a number of passionate Everton supporters who meticulously pointed out the mistakes which marred the Scot's tenure, it is only fair to bear witness to their reservations. 'He was a decent lad, but he bought us a lot of old crap,' observed one, offering the most critical opinion. Another told me: 'Walter Smith looked dead on his feet from the moment he arrived here, and he was knackered by the end of his first season. He didn't need a new challenge; he needed a rest.' A third perspective, provided by a Liverpool-based journalist, may be the most accurate: 'He was the wrong man in the wrong place. Everton had been steadily slipping further behind their city rivals, and there wasn't enough investment from the board to enable the manager to mount a revival. He didn't help his cause, mind you, by trying to shore up his team with old sweats like Duncan Ferguson, David Ginola and a clearly past-it Paul Gascoigne. The fans tolerated him and liked the guy – there was no problem with him – but when he was sacked in 2002, the new boy, David Moyes quickly proved that he had the youthful ambition which Smith lacked.' Perhaps it is significant that during his four-year period at Goodison, he did not attempt to lay down roots. That might explain why he seemed destined for the chop almost before the conclusion of his inaugural press conference.

A more painful deficiency in Smith's career review has been his lack of success in European competition, not least considering the lavish expenditure at his disposal, as David Murray strove to extend Rangers' dominance beyond domestic terrain. As soon as he assumed the mantle from Souness – after turning down a number of offers from him to move to Anfield – it was obvious to Smith that he required a larger number of Scottish-born personnel, given the limits being placed on foreign players in every squad. Sadly, the abiding memory of Rangers on Champions League duty in the 1990s was witnessing tales of woe, while Andy Goram produced a string of magnificent saves to restrict the damage to 3-0 or 4-0. These outcomes would inevitably prove the prelude to the usual suspects dashing into print to complain that the club had outgrown their origins, and that it was time for the Old Firm to migrate to Europe – a specious argument which nowadays tends to emanate more from Celtic Park, as if England's finest would be so ingenuous as to indulge in favours to rivals.

If the fans were chasing impossible dreams at that time and Smith did his utmost to live up to such grand ambitions, he was thwarted time and again by a queasy combination of superior opponents, tactical naivety, schoolboy howlers from his defenders and, whisper it, a lack of belief that the Ibrox men could seriously trouble the likes of Juventus. Whether this inferiority complex, which is not usually associated with Rangers teams, was the consequence of their relative inexperience in Europe's premier competition or whether Smith, so assured and confident in Scotland, suffered travel sickness when asked to plan strategies abroad, remains a matter of conjecture. I happen to believe that he had difficulties with the concept of assembling a squad who were capable of sustaining a twin-pronged attack. This should not be viewed with an excess of condemnation – Alex Ferguson has been as unconvincing in the role of Scotland manager as he has been magisterial in steering Aberdeen and Manchester United to European triumphs – but it does leave Smith exposed to the sniping of sceptics who pronounce that his domestic bullies wimped out at the highest level in his initial spell as manager.

Perhaps the most glaring manifestation of the tension bubbling constantly beneath the surface was the fundamental fashion in which Smith, usually a polite interviewee, lost his rag while fielding questions from BBC Scotland football journalist Chick Young, and launched into an expletive-laden tirade as the precursor to calling over assistant Archie Knox with the words: "Come and listen to this, Archie. Listen to the shite this wee c***'s coming out with." This clip, which has been screened across the world on the You Tube Internet service, should not be in the least shocking to those who attend football matches, but it is a significant episode for no other reason than that the look on Smith's face, amid his tantrums, reflects an amalgam of anger, frustration and resentment, all vying for primacy. 'People have raised this with me about 100 or 1,000 times now, and I really don't understand what all the fuss is about," says Young, who has laughed off similar spats with most of the high rollers in Scottish football. 'I asked Walter if he felt his players were good enough for Europe, and he took exception to the implication that somebody like Brian Laudrup was having his ability questioned, so there was a bit of industrial-strength language, but it was all done and dusted in the space of a few minutes, and soon enough we sat down and had a good laugh about it. The bottom line is that football is supposed to be a passionate business, and it would be boring if everybody agreed all the time. But I can honestly tell you there was no bad blood, no recriminations. That just isn't Walter Smith's style. The guy is an absolute gentleman, and I wager that you won't hear anything else from every section of the sport in Scotland."

I can testify to such unanimity, having spoken to Scottish managers of every discernible outlook. Even one such as Tommy Burns, who must have been shell-shocked at the fashion in which the Murray-Souness-Smith triumvirate laid waste to Celtic for much of the 1990s, talks about the Rangers man's honesty, his deep commitment to his country and his love for football with a directness which cannot be feigned. Perhaps the straightforward explanation is that Walter Smith has followed his own path and never sought greatness, but treated it with due respect when it has arrived. He carried out his duties in the wake of Jock Stein's untimely demise in 1985 or when Sir Alex Ferguson summoned him to Old Trafford in 2004, with the impassive relish of a character who fully appreciates that he might easily have ended up repairing electrical pylons if his life had veered a fraction in another direction.

Given which consideration, it is scarcely surprising that when Smith was showered with the accolade of Top Scot for 2006 in the Glenfiddich Spirit of Scotland Awards, he looked, initially at least, taken aback. It's all there in his expression: one fifth's worth of pride, a soupçon of incredulity, a further sprinkling of delight and an extra ingredient or two, of what? The realisation, as he knew well, that thousands of low-paid hospital staff and heroic fire-brigade crews had been saving lives every night across the country, without as much as a moment's thought from the Glenfiddich judging panel? The acknowledgement, however much he might love football and its infinitesimal mysteries, that he was being disproportionately rewarded for a solitary 1-0 success over France on a nerve-shredding afternoon, when the visitors to Glasgow might have been two goals in front in the opening half-hour? In the final analysis, however, Smith's celebratory humility struck the right note.

But then this is a trait that he shares with most of the best managers: an appreciation of the unsung heroes and a relish for those who carry out the regular chores without moaning about their lot. During his playing career Smith was a functional and prosaic performer, but nobody could ever accuse him of not expending 100 per cent of energy and desire. At Dundee United he watched the diverse methods of those on the Tannadice books, and though Smith can be as exhilarated by the flair of a Pele or Maradona as any observer, he is pragmatic enough to know that these players are rare in a Scottish context. Hence the manner in which Smith has praised the unstinting labours of Dundee United's Dougie Smith, a combative centre-half who joined the club in 1958, and who missed only four competitive matches in the next decade:

'He was a very quiet, very unassuming boy. He couldn't hold up a bunch of medals or anything like that at the end of his career.

But I don't think I've known many people who wanted to win as much as he did. His personality wasn't always what people would hold up as being a winner's, but he definitely had a winning attitude. It was etched in him, this fierce hunger to win. A lot of times players run around kicking people and shouting at referees, and people view that as a desire to win. But Dougie didn't do that. The desire was within him, and it burned very brightly. It taught me that there are guys who maybe don't have a lot of ability who can bring themselves up to a tremendous level in any sport, and though they may just fall short of winning, in their own right they are actually winners, because they have dragged themselves up from being not the most naturally gifted to being amongst the best, and I really admire that. In fact, in some respects, in doing so they may have almost achieved more than some people who win medals. It might not look that way from outside, but a lot of managers in football do a terrific job without getting an end product in terms of trophies or championships.'

Walter Smith's words are significant. They confirm that he has never had patience with those inclined to abuse their talent or to spend greater time at the nightclub than attending to the day job. This is an inevitable reflection of his upbringing, and we have heard the references to how Celtic supporters, asked to choose their club's greatest-ever player, plumped for a prodigiously talented tanner-ba' trickster known as Jimmy Johnstone. The Rangers brethren, by comparison, when presented with the same choice, hummed and hawed at Archie Henderson and Colin Stein, Davie Cooper and Archie Conn before settling for John Greig, an admittedly effective and aggressive defender who possessed all the romance and magic of a knee-trembler in Maryhill. On reflection, while the selection of Greig provoked sarcastic abuse around Celtic Park, he was a genuinely populist choice. Few of the supporters who flocked to Old Firm tussles in the 1960s could possibly have conceived of executing the mesmerising feints and

jinks which were Johnstone's trademarks. In contrast, all in the
Rangers ranks could easily have imagined themselves lunging
at Jinky and kicking him into the middle of Row C. A brutal
distinction, admittedly, but Greig was built in the classic Ibrox
tradition, namely: if you're looking for frills or fancy-dan stuff, go
elsewhere. That robust militarism, the ingrained philosophy of
'Take no prisoners' ensured that while he was nobody's idea of a
stylist, the young Walter Smith watched John Greig in action –
and cheered.

In that respect, on the long and winding road from Ashfield
Juniors to Tannadice and Dumbarton, prior to being instrumental
in the Rangers revolution and from there onwards to Everton,
and eventually to unemployment, Smith's exploits have all been of
the understated variety, and he has never been a man to indulge in
trumpet-blowing. Yet for me, the working-class dignity that he
has invariably exuded is redolent of the best Scottish values.
When the call came from the SFA, when seeking a saviour in the
worst days of the Vogts-inspired morass, it would have been the
comfortable option to decline their offer and to continue ponti-
ficating on the periphery as an occasional pundit, but the easy
outcome has rarely appealed. Instead, in his late 50s and safe in
the knowledge that he had masterminded 13 trophies in seven
seasons at Ibrox, he grabbed the challenge by the scruff of the
neck, united myriad factions within the Tartan Army, and galvanised the Scotland side with such basic qualities as discipline,
pride in the jersey and organisation. There was no mystery to it,
but just as he has done at Rangers since replacing Paul le Guen,
Smith has shown that home-spun industry need not be inferior to
foreign methods.

Whether he is a good manager with a gifted streak, or a great
motivator with a shop steward's ability to motivate the troops, is
open to debate. But those who have worked with him and
absorbed the lessons he has imparted, are in no doubt as to
his status. 'One thing I will say about him is that he is a gentleman,
but if you get on the wrong side of him, he will quickly let you

know,' notes Charlie Nicholas, an individual one might suppose, as a media-friendly, Celtic-supporting dandy, was everything alien to Smith. 'I worked with him when he was Alex Ferguson's assistant at the 1986 World Cup finals in Mexico, and I had five weeks with him, and he displayed a burning intensity throughout that period. Scotland mattered so, so much to him, and that couldn't help but filter through to the players. When I heard he had taken the Scotland job in 2004, I was mightily relieved, because I knew he wouldn't tolerate a situation where a country with our history was languishing at 77th in the FIFA rankings. And you have to give him credit: he stamped his authority on the team and made a strong impression on the youngsters, and the turnaround was almost immediate. That tells you a lot about the man's ambition.' Typically, Smith is not interested in hogging the limelight, to the extent that even the hapless Vogts escapes his wrath in this summation:

'Let's be fair. It was a very, very difficult time for Berti to take the job. Craig Brown had been in charge of a very settled Scottish squad, but a lot of them were getting older, and those of us who were involved in football in Scotland knew that there were not a lot of guys around who were ready to take their place, so it was never going to be easy. Coming from another country, perhaps Berti didn't quite realise the scale of those difficulties. And there is a different mentality in British football, and I think he maybe found that hard to encompass as well. The thing is, when Scotland had players of the calibre of Denis Law, Billy Bremner, Graeme Souness, Alan Hansen and Kenny Dalglish, the team pretty much picked itself. But when you don't have players of that quality, the mentality of the players you pick comes far more into it, and it helps if you know the personality of the lads you are dealing with. It's maybe why you don't see many foreign managers taking over at places like Coventry and Southampton, where you have to build from the bottom up. When they come to Britain, they tend to come to big clubs with top players.'

Smith has been associated with many notable names in his vocation, and he has thrived in the company of lesser-known individuals, such as Jerry Kelly at Dundee United and the ubiquitous Archie Knox on their peripatetic trail. Though he is not inclined to hero-worship, there is little question which other Glasgow figure he holds in the highest eminence:

'The obvious fact that I know and have worked with Sir Alex maybe makes me a wee bit biased, but when you talk about creating a winning environment, there has been nobody better in my experience. It isn't just what he has done at Manchester United, who are an enormous club, but also at Aberdeen. They are not as powerful a club as Rangers or Celtic, but he still managed to turn them into a side who won a European trophy, who weren't afraid to tackle the Old Firm, and made them a team who were always incredibly difficult to beat. So, probably he more than anybody else is the man I admire and respect in our sport.'

Life has been one of ebb-and-flow for Walter Smith since he entered this world on 24 February 1948. His critics too readily condemn his perceived fortune in being privy to David Murray's riches, and Rangers fans gorged on success so consistently throughout the 1990s that they assumed his regular acquisition of silverware would carry on with or without him in the boiler-room. The trick for Smith now will be to prove that he can orchestrate another piece of astute stewardship in a very different climate. Only a fool or a mystic would dismiss him lightly. Not just because Rangers pulsates in his blood, but because he vividly remembers those who perished on the stairs in 1971, and he has pledged to do whatever he can to erase the stains of that tragedy.

CHAPTER TWO

GROWING UP IN FOOTBALL
AND LIFE ITSELF

❖

'He was a good, hard-working Scottish defender'

As Walter Smith is fond of reminding friends, there was a place for every footballer, irrespective of talent, size or commitment, among the fraternity of post-war schoolchildren who grew up addicted to the sport in Glasgow in the 1950s. Move forward to a new century, and it may seem strange to youngsters that their Scottish predecessors could have been so easily impressed. While it would be wrong to paint an overly sentimental picture of a period when gang warfare was rife and when a criminal dubbed Bible John was indulging in murderous exploits against women, a sense of shared community and *esprit de corps* were evident. The youthful Smith wrapped himself in football to the extent that every waking moment, when he wasn't at school, he surrounded himself with comics, match programmes and newspaper features on his beloved Rangers, and he dared to dream that one day he might sprint on to the Ibrox greensward. As he came to realise even before he had reached teenage years, he boasted the commitment, but not the class, the enthusiasm but not the extra ingredient which marks out the elite from the journeymen, and he resolved to progress as far as he could without being deluded by the idea that he was on a par with John Greig or Colin Stein.

There was no shame in that acceptance. The opposite, because Glasgow at that time was fixated with three things: football, heavy industry and religion. Smith could do nothing about two of those factors, but the sport was another matter. In common with thousands of his contemporaries, he was hooked.

As he related recently, the die was cast from his first fleeting experiences. Every Saturday and Sunday, wherever he and his mates could find pitches, the sole thought was to organise matches of six-a-side, 11-a-side or 22-a-side. Who cared, so long as there was the opportunity to break the monotony with a trip to dreamland? The weather, the state of the facilities and prospect of exams were rendered irrelevant, and though Smith was no class-room dullard – he shared with Alex Ferguson the capacity to soak up general knowledge like blotting paper – he was content to be captivated by his favourite game, as Glasgow lived up to its billing as the first city of football. It was, quite simply, another world, a vanished sphere of rudimentary pleasures. Many youngsters in the 21st century appear lost without mobile phones, PlayStations and other sophisticated devices, but the ground rules were much more straightforward in the formative Smith years. If it snowed and then froze, as it frequently did, he and his comrades would use sand to mark out impromptu pitches; if it rained, they would clamber over walls and sneak into car parks and school premises, and kick lumps out of one another on concrete or tarmac. Luxuries extended to the occasional Christmas present of a spanking new strip or a leather ball, and this down-to-earth upbringing was evident in the home: for much of the 1950s people were considered pretty posh if they owned a television and had a telephone. As for other items which we now take for granted – microwave ovens, video recorders, refrigerators and washing machines – Smith and his childhood contemporaries would have thought the Martians had landed if they had stumbled across any of these contraptions in the east end of Glasgow.

Even if it was a basic upbringing, Smith revelled in it. 'I was as keen as anybody else when I was a kid, and I went where the games were,' he recalls. 'It's the same with everyone, isn't it? You want a game, you are desperate to play, and you follow the rest of the lads in your group just to make sure that you are playing football somewhere.' At the outset, this entailed the two best performers convening the others and picking their best pals, whereupon they would move down the line until just a couple of duffers were left. In some respects this was a cruel process of elimination, but it was effective, and lest anyone forget, Smith grew up in a halcyon period for Scottish football, an era when the Old Firm, Hibernian, Heart of Midlothian and Dundee all celebrated rousing European adventures, and posted some momentous wins against the best on the Continent. Across the country, but most notably in Glasgow, every tiny strip of land was a home to wannabe Jimmy Johnstones and John Greigs, and as Craig Brown, the former Scotland manager, recollects, the competition for places at every level, from juvenile and junior to amateur and professional, was relentless: 'In these days, you could travel round Glasgow at weekends, and on every street corner there were laddies chasing a ball for dear life, while the parks, whether they were blaes or grass or ash, were always packed out.' Brown offers the noteworthy observation that Scottish children in those days received 10 sessions of physical education, hence the avoidance of the chronic obesity which has crept into our vocabulary in the past 20 years. 'Most of us who love football know that we will never see a situation such as that again – there are too many other distractions for kids and a lot of the old playing fields have been swallowed up by developers – but although there was no shortage of problems in Scotland 50–60 years ago, there was also something heart-warming about being in an environment where football was king.'

Less admirable was the bitter sectarian divide which existed in the west of Scotland, and guaranteed that most of Smith's generation strolled unquestioningly into the blue or green camp, often without recognising the more nefarious elements that inhabited such a culture. Even with hindsight, it seems extraordinary that so many lives should have been wasted on this issue, let alone that an appalling degree of ignorance often lies at the heart of the most deep-rooted bigotry. In the years when I grew up in West Lothian, on the edge of the Harthill Triangle which veered into the fastnesses of Lanarkshire, I noticed the graffiti on the walls between Whitburn and the Polkemmet Estate:

'Kaflix are Skum,' declared one legend. 'Protistants are Kunts,' was one response.

Along the road at regular intervals the letters 'FTP' had been spray-painted with finesse sufficient to stimulate thoughts that the perpetrator might do well on an art course, rather than wasting the talent on insulting the man in charge at the Vatican. Once, while walking from the estate to the relative civilisation of my home town, I was stopped by a couple of wild-eyed men who pinned me against a wall and demanded to know my religion. 'Protestant,' I blurted out, which was apparently the correct answer, since they did not beat me to a pulp. Earlier, as a primary-school laddie I was in the act of buying my *Victor* comic from the newsagent's on what happened to be the day of the famous European Cup final involving Celtic and Inter Milan. The shop owner, Jim Hamilton, a rubicund chap sporting blue-nose and red-nose propensities, and with an unnerving ability to snivel and shout at the same time, adopted the role of chief interrogator and defender of the faith:

'So what team are you supporting?'
   'Er, well I want Celtic to win.'
   'Why's that?'
   'Because they are Scottish, Mr Hamilton.'
   'Aye, but they are Catholics, son.'
   'Yes, but aren't the other team Catholics as well?'
   'That disnae matter – they are *foreign* Catholics! Now that'll be thruppence, please.'

This was perhaps bigotry of a minor character, but almost 20 years later one of my occasional Catholic football-playing colleagues fatally stabbed one of his Protestant workmates in a drunken brawl that was precipitated by an argument over the Old Firm, and he found himself behind bars for the rest of his active life. All of which testifies to my belief that, long after drawing-room pontificators have lost interest in the subject, sectarianism will continue to be a blight on Scotland and the west of the nation, in particular, perhaps not around Ibrox and Celtic Park, where security and policing have eliminated most of the trouble, but more probably through random outbreaks of violence and hostilities, sparking agony for communities in Ayrshire, Lanarkshire and West Lothian. Within these areas I know of families who won't allow their children to dress in green, or even use a crayon of that colour. Similarly, I am acquainted with one or two Celtic followers who casually make jokes about the Ibrox Disaster or strive to defend the Enniskillen bombings during the troubles in Northern Ireland, while striving to refute my argument that Aiden McGeady, who was born and bred in Scotland to Scottish parents and who established his reputation by playing for a Scottish club, should be honoured to represent Scotland, instead of trotting out words such as history and tradition to justify his decision to aspire to international honours with the Republic of Ireland.

In circumstances which inspire such enigmatic episodes, it would be unsurprising if Walter Smith had not been dragged into the ritual bigotry which used to tarnish Glasgow on Old Firm derby afternoons, and which was brilliantly depicted in Peter MacDougall's *Just Another Saturday*. Yet to his credit, he has managed to transcend tribal conflict by adopting the mantra: 'Treat people as you find them'. Even as a teenager, when he turned out for Chapelhall Youth Club while studying for an apprenticeship at Coatbridge Tech, Smith was blessed with the knack of being able to make friends on gut feeling, not after checking what educational establishment or church his new ally had attended. Time and again his only priority lay in being part of a team, whether at Chapelhall or the Albert Youth Club in Springburn, or after joining Bishopbriggs Amateurs at the age of 17. Smith soon stepped up to the junior ranks at Ashfield in the company of team-mates Jim Cameron and Gerry Hernon. Suddenly he was in demand, and though there was no sign of scouts from Rangers, Smith was astonishingly pragmatic for one of his age. He ignored the idea that football might offer him full-time employment, and bolstered by his father he chose to conclude his apprenticeship before contemplating his next stage in life. He devoted himself to his five-year stint, first at Dalmarnock Power Station for the South of Scotland Electricity Board, and one former co-employee told me: 'Walter was intense. He was anxious to pick up as much as he could, and I wager he would still know what to do if he suffered a power cut at home. He would come into work and talk about football over a cup of tea. But once that was finished and his shift had begun, he was only interested in doing his job.' Those words epitomise the Smith philosophy. Ally McCoist once jested that his gaffer had walked into Ibrox with the hair of Sacha Distel, and had departed with that of Steve Martin, such was the stress he had experienced within the goldfish bowl. But Smith has always been naturally meticulous, intense and disinclined to laziness, all of which makes him awkward company for time-wasters. Craig Brown, a friend for more than 30 years, sums him up:

'Walter was one of the most driven and enthusiastic people you could hope to meet, right from the early days. It was as if he knew that while he might not reach the top of the tree as a player, there was no reason why he couldn't use his intelligence and his football knowledge to make an impression as a leader, a coach, a manager. What you have to appreciate is that while Walter, and to some extent Sir Alex Ferguson, might give the impression that they are pretty gruff individuals, the truth is they are very droll characters, who can deliver a punch-line perfectly when the mood takes them.

Another factor in their success is the fact that both are incredibly competitive characters – they hate losing, utterly detest it, and we're not talking here about matches, but games of Trivial Pursuit on the bus!

'Whenever we were on Scotland duty together, the pair of them would start their quizzes, and I suppose it boils down to the old Scottish notion of the lad o' pairts. So if Fergie was able to name every member of the cast of *The Magnificent Seven*, then Walter would come back at him with the list of actors in *The Great Escape*. They have been like that for as long as I can remember: ultra-competitive men, fiercely-passionate folk who enjoy their successes, but suffer their defeats as much as any fan. And they share the notion that genius is an infinite capacity for taking pains.'

❖

By the stage that Smith had joined Ashfield Juniors in August 1966, he had demonstrated that what he lacked in class as a defender was compensated for by lashings of sinew and purpose. Such was the impact that he made at Saracen Park, the home of his new junior colleagues, that within a couple of months he had been recruited by Dundee United's stalwart manager, Jerry Kerr, on the old provisional signing forms. Smith spent most of that subsequent season alternating between fulfilling his commitments to Ashfield, turning out in reserve matches for the Tannadice club and completing his trade apprenticeship at the Dundee-based company, Loudon Brothers, where he worked full-time while embarking on gruelling training sessions in the evening. It sounds an anachronistic means of pursuing a football career, and many were the nights when Smith was dead-beat even before entering the changing rooms, but he recalls that he was young, fit and ambitious, and the alternative was an anonymous existence surrounded by crossed wires and short circuits. And yet the question hangs in the air: if Smith was able to secure a deal as a teenager with Dundee United, could he have been as lacklustre a performer as he claims? 'I was ordinary, very ordinary. And I am not being in the least modest when I tell you that,' he retorts. 'Over the period I played for Dundee United, I like to think that I developed into a good pro, and I did look after my fitness, but in truth almost from the start I knew that, much as I loved the game, I was never going to be any great shakes as a player.' Craig Brown offers a different assessment of his colleague: 'Walter was much better than what you might believe from hearing him dismiss his career. He was a good centre-half, he read the game well, expended lots of energy, and he tackled for keeps. If he had a failing, it lay in his lack of mobility, and obviously once he began picking up injuries, that didn't help him at the highest level. But it is plain wrong to describe him as some sort of donkey; more accurate to conclude that he was a good, hard-working Scottish defender, who coped well in the domestic leagues without aiming any higher.'

What is not in doubt is that Smith's migration to Tayside was the best move he could have made. Away from his roots he thrived under the influence of Jerry Kerr, a sharp-suited, pipe-smoking polymath who seemed to belong in another age. When Smith arrived, he witnessed the swansong of the Swede, Lennart Wing, and he recognised that the club, buoyed by such tireless servants as Tommy Millar, Denis Gillespie and his icon Doug Smith, were set to supplant near-neighbours Dundee as the No1 team in the city, not least because the wily Kerr was a past master at snapping up veterans with one or two more prolific seasons still in them. All of which ensured that Smith was quickly enjoying experiences that he could only have dreamt about back in Carmyle and Springburn. At the end of his first season in 1968, Dundee United travelled to the United States with a clutch of other representatives from Scotland and England, in a concerted attempt to sell round ball football to an obdurate American public. The Brits were unsuccessful in that objective, but Smith was in his element while turning out for the Dallas Tornados and settling down comfortably in the Texan city, relishing the lifestyle that was lavished on the British missionaries. This experience did not last, but Smith prospered briefly in the United States, returning to Scotland with the notion that anything was possible and enthused by the fashion in which Kerr rebuilt his side to meet their rising aspirations. He was bolstered by the advice and comradeship of Millar, who had witnessed almost every idiosyncrasy which football can deliver, and he learned important lessons from Gillespie and Alan Gordon, who had signed from Hibs, thanks to the trademark eye for a main chance which characterised Kerr. Smith wrote in 1994:

'Things were different back then, and Jerry was probably the last of the old-fashioned managers. I say that in the nicest possible way, because Jerry was a remarkable manager for Dundee United. Indeed, it's almost impossible to criticise him after what he did for the Tannadice club. He built the main stand, he took them into the top league, and he kept them there during his time as boss [1959–71]. And he took them into Europe, where they beat Barcelona, frightened the life out of Juventus, and made United known outside their country for the first time in their history.

'But his style of management was from an era which was dying out when I went to United as a professional. The age of the track-suited manager was in its infancy in Scotland, and Jerry was completely untouched by it. He ran the club, he picked the team and he bought the players, and then he allowed them to get on with the tactics by themselves. He never took training, and was always dressed in a collar and tie and usually a suit, but the bottom line is that he was successful, and he deserves credit for that.'

Kerr's achievements reflect the wind of change that swept through Tannadice as the 1960s progressed. A product of Armadale in West Lothian, his playing career included spells at Motherwell, Alloa Athletic, Edinburgh club St Bernard's and Dundee United before he briefly turned out for Rangers after the Second World War, but it was in the sphere of management that his radical ideas bore fruit. Equipped with the theory that the bigger the club the worse their talent-spotting, he insisted on a full-time structure at United, was adamant there should be a properly constituted reserve side, and abandoned the policy of relying on parochial, probably over-the-hill talent. Instead, with Morton FC's Hal Stewart he tapped into the flourishing Scandinavian football scene, and purchased a string of cultured performers at affordable prices: Mogens Berg, Lennart Wing and Orjan Persson were among those who provided sterling service for Scottish employers. Kerr, though, was not one whose life revolved around football exclusively, and he relished cricket with equal enthusiasm. He had watched with curiosity as Warwickshire County Cricket Club raised thousands of pounds for rebuilding their Edgbaston ground in Birmingham by establishing their own pools structure. Kerr, a bright man who was always happy to seek advice, engaged with county secretary Les Deakin, and the consequence was the creation of Taypools, which proved an instant success and brought significant sums of money into Dundee United's coffers by the end of the decade. Given the dynamism and bristling sense of purpose which this livewire engendered, few Taysiders were surprised when he marched his Tangerine warriors into Europe for the first time in 1966, and they swept to an astonishing 4-1 aggregate victory over Barcelona, including a 2-1 triumph at the Nou Camp. This was the environment into which the youthful Walter Smith had advanced, and during the next decade he soaked up loads of inspiration to good effect. Little wonder that when Jerry Kerr died in 1999 aged 87, Smith was among the first to pay tribute to the methods and mystique of a hero whose achievements remained largely unsung.

CHAPTER THREE

A Coach in the Making

❖

'Wattie was the guy who kept the spirits up'

One of Walter Smith's great joys is the camaraderie of the training ground, which is central to the crucial transformation of a group of young men from a collection of disparate individuals into a solid fighting unit. Every squad will possess their gregarious types and their loners, those who enjoy their alcohol too fondly and who fret that they don't belong, and those who feel homesick and perhaps suspect that they are not part of the manager's plans. In fostering harmony, the leaders of such men must quell restless spirits without dampening their fire, combine equal proportions of comedy, common sense and cantankerousness, and be able to persuade each man, from first-team superstar to grafter, that they have a unique role to act out in a championship challenge. Smith has long appreciated that there is no magic formula to the process. After signing with Dundee United in 1966 and gradually earning respect from Jerry Kerr, he struggled to command a regular first-team position, a situation which he accepted with the knowledge that the manager had assembled a fine ensemble of performers, and that if he had to settle for bit-part status, so be it. One of the rewards of charting Smith's rise to the highest level, though, is recognising the fortitude that he displayed while lingering around the periphery on so many weekends, apparently consigned to the substitutes' bench. In parallel with what appears often to have been a thankless exercise, he took the opportunity to sharpen his tactical acumen and to embrace the positives.

Had he been a wastrel who was disposed to slip away from training or a prima donna who was disinclined to carry out reserve duty, surely Smith would not have flourished when Kerr handed over the reins of Dundee United to Jim McLean in 1971. But he did. And McLean, no matter those facets of his personality which could be described as thrawn, impatient, unreasonable or plain grumpy, achieved more in his 22-year spell as manager than any individual before or after. From the outset, as a bustling and redoubtable 34-year-old who had been in charge at Dundee FC, and was damned sure he would not cross the barricades only to come a cropper, the not-so-sunny Jim barked out instructions with a relentless beat, but his tactics had the desired result. The club's fitness regime was intensified, training grew ever more organised with longer sessions and an evident emphasis on strategy, and Smith, who was already considering a future in football after he retired from the playing arena, was immediately impressed by the new boss. This was in contrast to several United stalwarts, who actively resisted the changes and argued that Mr Kerr's notions suited them better – and were rapidly destined for the Tannadice exit.

As it happened, Smith decided to move on in 1975, for a spell with Dumbarton, and the decision owed much to McLean's determination to construct a new young team, which he could mould in his own image. For all that he admired the unstinting work ethic and resilience exhibited by Smith, a worthy defender was by now excess to requirements. There was nothing untoward about the temporary split, and the two men were reunited at Tannadice in 1977, by which time Smith's playing career was winding down on account of a pelvic injury, though he did not make his 250th, and final, senior appearance for United until 1980.

This proved to be a pivotal period in the history of the Scottish game. At the start of the 1970s, the Old Firm continued to dominate their Scottish rivals and Celtic reached their second European Cup final, only to be surprisingly vanquished by Feyenoord, while Rangers triumphed in the 1972 European Cup-Winners' Cup. Despite the processional fashion in which Jock Stein's Celtic accumulated nine consecutive titles and their Glasgow rivals clung on to end the stranglehold in 1975, changes were afoot in the shape of novel ideas and the unearthing of a new generation of aspirational managers. In some respects, figures such as Alex Ferguson, Craig Brown, Andy Roxburgh, Jim McLean, and eventually Walter Smith, were assisted by the deficiencies within Scottish football at the highest echelons, a malaise confirmed by grim recollections of World Cup campaigns, which were laced with embarrassment and amateurism. Much has been made of the 1978 finals fiasco in Argentina, where manager Ally MacLeod failed properly to analyse his squad's opponents, and a national hangover of monumental proportions followed. But if the opprobrium heaped upon MacLeod was merited, the SFA were exposed as a bunch of mediocrities, who seemed to many observers to be more concerned with checking themselves and their wives into high-class accommodation, while the poor bloody infantry of players were consigned to lodgings that were much inferior. Looking further back to the 1974 World Cup, Willie Ormond, a likeable and engaging chap with an enormous soccer talent but with limited managerial skills, had found himself out of his depth, while the SFA seemed satisfied that their team had excelled by merely reaching the tournament finals.

Beyond such trials and tribulations, Smith was offered a platform to hone his tactical skills, and he grabbed the opportunity. After his return to Dundee United, Jim McLean eased him into a coaching role in which he worked with S-form youngsters for a few hours every week, and examination of the list of youngsters that he instructed, including Davie Dodds, John Clark, Dave Beaumont and Maurice Malpas, confirms the quality that was emerging at the grass-roots. Not only was he demonstrating his worth at Tannadice: he had gained employment with the Scottish youth team, who would go on to conquer Europe. From the age of 25, Smith had ventured to the SFA's coaching courses at Largs, sitting exams and gaining certificates with as much resolve as he had entered into tackles on the pitch. Craig Brown, who was instrumental in presenting the courses with Willie McLean and Peter Rice, pinpoints that dedication:

'Walter was one of the best students you could imagine. He listened, he learned, he asked questions, and if there was something he didn't understand, he would come to us later and find out what he wanted to know. It was a fantastic time to be involved, as we moved into the 1980s. The Old Firm's aura of invincibility had been shattered by the emergence of so many good players at Aberdeen and Dundee United, and you sensed that life was going to be exciting in the future. At youth level, there was a rich seam of guys making their mark, people of the calibre of Ally McCoist, Charlie Nicholas, Eric Black, Pat Nevin, Brian McClair, Jim McInally, Dave Bowman . . . The list goes on, and all these boys were determined to reach the top of their profession – it was no longer just a game for these lads – so there was no problem with motivating them. As soon as Walter entered the scene, his eyes lit up and he recognised that there could be big things in store with this amount of raw potential at his disposal. And true to form, he pressed the buttons and clicked the right gears.'

Irrespective of the opposition, Jim McLean's teams learned to prosper, and they displayed a good deal of panache and derring-do in doing so, the product of endless hours of coaxing and cajoling by the manager. In December 1979 he guided the club to a Scottish League Cup triumph, and retained the trophy the following year. Meanwhile, United were amassing a sequence of wins against European sides, among them AS Monaco, PSV Eindhoven, Anderlecht, Werder Bremen and Borussia Moenchengladbach, whose cumulative effect ensured that continental coaches and players started to fear a date with the men from

Tayside. As for Walter Smith, who had slipped seamlessly into the No. 2 job at Tannadice, there was no mystery about the club's surge, which saw them secure the Scottish championship in 1983:

'Jim was one of the most thorough managers you could ever meet. And I mean anywhere. I don't care where you go. It would be hard to find anyone who put more into planning for games and for training sessions than he did. That was always one of his great secrets, namely that he would leave nothing to chance. His tactics when going into specific games were worked out to the very last detail. And his own discipline, and the discipline which he imposed on other people, was very tough to live up to. But he demanded that, and he always led by example.'

In tandem with Andy Roxburgh, Smith had adapted well to the requirements of coaching his young charges at Scotland level, and the distillation of their labours was a great victory in the European Youth Championship in 1982 in Finland, where they saw off the challenges of England, the Netherlands, Czechoslovakia, Poland, Turkey and Albania with a mix of traditional values, which included robust defence, wholehearted commitment and playing for the jersey. This was combined with a high-tempo, attacking style which perplexed many of their rivals, but constituted no surprise to those who had studied the emergence of Dundee United under McLean, and Aberdeen under Alex Ferguson. One of Smith's few regrets in looking back at the event was the realisation that only three members of a gifted Scottish squad, Paul McStay, Pat Nevin and Gary Mackay, went on to gain full international honours. If that failure to translate teenage flair into adult fruition remains a dilemma for Scotland, it was no fault of Smith, whose stature in the game rose significantly after the triumph of his youthful charges. Mackay recalls:

'Andy was in charge, but Wattie was the guy who kept the spirits up and organised all the activities which you need when you are away from home for ten days. He was second-in-command, but he kept the players bright and alert and positive about themselves. He had been involved in the build-up and had helped develop the squad over the course of the season, and it was a particularly strong group of players, with guys like McStay, Nevin, Ally Dick and Neale Cooper, although Neale missed the finals because he was involved with Aberdeen. But the bottom line is that you can have a collection of good players, but unless they are drilled properly and trained properly and they care about one another, they won't amount to much, and that is where Wattie came into his own. He and Andy both stressed the importance of the team ethic, but they also allowed individual exuberance to flourish, and getting the blend right was one of the reasons why we won the tournament. I will always remember what Wattie said on the Saturday night before the final. England had just beaten Scotland 1-0 in the Home International Championship at Hampden Park, and he told us this wasn't just a chance for us to make a name for ourselves, but also an opportunity to dispel the disappointment of the whole nation. He was passionate, his eyes were burning, but he was really inspiring, and that fired us all up for the job.'

Smith was a mere 34, but most of the qualities which would earn him a plethora of plaudits later in his career had manifested themselves. As he surveyed the Scots dismantle the Czechs 3-1 in the final, with goals from Mackay, Nevin and Stirling Albion's John Philliben, the click of his jaw and leap in the air at the climax told its own story of a joyful campaign. He came over as a calm, stoical presence on the touchline, but disagreeing with him could set off volcanic responses, and the intensity of Smith's wrath left hardened men quaking. While several former players told me of how he had allegedly challenged them to put their fists up or shut up, none would speak on the record, not least because as one explained: 'Walter was right. I was being a prick, and I needed a slap. He only lost the rag if he thought you were letting the side or yourself down. And I was able to laugh about it with him the next day. But believe me, when he felt he had to crack the whip, he was bloody fearsome.'

Away from Tannadice, seismic cracks were beginning to appear in Glasgow, which would eventually have major repercussions for Smith and Scottish football. With Dundee United securing the league title and Aberdeen subsequently recording a magnificent 2-1 victory over Real Madrid on a sodden night in Gothenburg to collect the European Cup-Winners' Cup, the balance of power had shifted markedly away from the Old Firm and at Rangers, as their supporters showed their disaffection in a flood of fickleness and an embarrassment of empty seats, manager John Greig left his office in the autumn to the unfamiliar sound of booing from those who had once saluted him (and indeed would acclaim him as their hero again in the future). Alex Ferguson was sounded out to replace Greig, but the redoubtable Glaswegian declined, principally on the grounds that he had witnessed at first hand the pernicious effects of sectarianism, and considered it anathema that Rangers, publicly at least, adhered to their policy of refusing to sign Roman Catholic players. Several had turned out for the club, including John Spencer, but discrimination hung in the air, and Ferguson, despite being made an offer that many individuals could not have refused, remained at Pittodrie. Next up Jim McLean was invited to speak to the Rangers board, and in the course of the initial meeting informed the directors that he intended to bring Smith with him to Ibrox. There was no discussion between the men, McLean assuming correctly that his No. 2 would be cock-a-hoop at the prospect of a move to the club that he had supported from childhood. The deal seemed cut and dried, but no sooner had newspapers started to debate how best the new management team could extricate Rangers from the mire, than McLean, normally such a purposeful character, slipped into procrastination. He asked Smith for his opinion, receiving an unequivocal response: 'Let's go for it.' He decided to sleep on the matter for a night, followed by another, and despite keeping his counsel, it was obvious that McLean was harbouring misgivings. At the beginning of the following week, with one or two Rangers officials furious at how the affair was unravelling, he announced forcefully to Smith that they were definitely going to Ibrox: he had communicated that message to the Dundee United chairman, Johnstone Grant. Yet it proved another false dawn. On Friday morning a board meeting was held at Tannadice at 10 a.m. rather than the usual midday, and as a small group of players sat in the dressing room just before noon, a senior director, George Fox, marched in to confirm that McLean was staying where he was, as was his No. 2.

It was a crushing blow for Smith. He could not comprehend why there had been so much hesitation from a man he had always held in the highest regard; there was no explanation from his colleague why he had blown hot and cold over the move; and by proxy, Smith had spurned his beloved club, and surely could forget any notion of being handed another chance in future. His reaction to Fox's announcement was carried through on auto-pilot. Have a shower. Get dressed. Bite lip forcibly. Jump into car and drive away as quickly as possible. Ignore the press. Draw a veil over the business, and continue to be professional. After all, he was still in employment with the Scottish champions. In the intervening period, little clarification has come to light to explain McLean's ultimate reticence. One theory is that he felt he could not be seen to embrace Rangers' non-Catholic signing policy, which he considered an anachronism, especially as he had signed many talented Catholics for Dundee United. A less credible proposition is that McLean believed that he should have been in the frame for the Rangers job ahead of the less experienced Ferguson. There again, as one who had regularly voiced his concerns over the excessive influence that the Old Firm held over Scottish football, perhaps he indulged in private intrigue at Rangers' expense. Or more cynically, McLean, who had always commanded a Napoleonic sway in Dundee, perhaps could not tolerate the idea of having to delegate power or deal with genuine superstars, who would not be content to be treated as chattels on six-year contracts or risk having wages docked after winning a match 6-0 because they had relaxed in the final 20 minutes, as happened at United. Whatever the reason – and it may be that McLean simply decided that he and his family were perfectly happy with life in the environs of Broughty Ferry – he has not voiced any regrets. But then there *is* life beyond the Old Firm.

Smith and his manager remained friends, but the relationship had altered perceptibly from avuncular to merely amiable. One long-serving Rangers official says: 'All through his career, Walter Smith has done his best to avoid fall-outs with other people, and has largely succeeded. That's not to say he is a soft touch, far from it, but there is a sentimental streak beneath the gruffness: he really wants to think the best of folk, and if he is disappointed in that judgment, he is really disappointed. So I can imagine that he would have been devastated by what happened with Jim McLean, but he wasn't going to spill his guts to the press or go looking for confrontation. That's not him at all.' As it was, Smith and McLean were travelling towards a fork in the road, and the younger man had resolved that if he received an offer from a leading club he would not stick around in someone's shadow. He had all but relinquished hope that Rangers would come calling anew, but then life is full of surprises, some of them tragic.

CHAPTER FOUR

Intriguing Duo Answer Call to Ibrox

❖

'He was a perfect foil for Graeme Souness'

After years of striving hard behind the scenes, Walter Smith suddenly burst into the public eye at the end of 1985. The circumstances were not as he would have wished, and Scots and followers of football across the globe were left numbed when Jock Stein collapsed and died at the end of Scotland's World Cup qualifying match against Wales in Cardiff. The tearful scenes that followed the demise of the national team's charismatic manager ensured that Scotland's bid to make the finals in Mexico became even more charged, as they faced a play-off over two legs against Australia. The SFA installed Alex Ferguson as stand-in manager with Smith as his deputy, accompanied by a coaching staff of Archie Knox, Andy Roxburgh and Craig Brown. A routine 2-0 Scottish victory brought goals from Davie Cooper and Frank McAvennie in the first leg, though the team's failure to secure a decisive third strike rankled with a few supporters. But on the night of 20 November most of the Tartan Army were too wrapped up in the emotion of the occasion to care that much. Many were still in mourning for the Big Man, and Ferguson, who was normally so masterful when dealing with an Aberdeen team that he had nurtured for much of the previous decade, fretted over tinkering with his predecessor's squad. Indeed, when the Scots travelled to Australia, some of the players spoke of the air of unreality which pervaded their mission, epitomised by Ferguson's decision to depart the squad to visit a relative, and it was as if they all wished they could all be somewhere else. Smith, though, took charge of the players with an assurance which demonstrated the techniques that he had assimilated from his stimulating association with Scotland's youths. Recognising that the worst thing he could do, in the sweltering temperatures of Melbourne, was to adopt a heavy-handed approach by enforcing an excess of training sessions, he granted the tour party a day off, and the players were offered the opportunity of a round of golf or heading to the races. Former international goalkeeper Alan Rough fills in the fascinating details of a golf story and its aftermath:

'The only proviso was that we had to be back in our hotel by teatime, because we had been invited to attend a function by a group of local expatriates, and the management had lent their blessing to the proposal. So it was that Graeme Sharp, David Speedie and I popped off to a nearby golf course, and the thought that we might suffer in the heat hardly crossed our minds. Our round started at 11 a.m. with 100 degrees already showing on the thermometer, and it climbed by another 10 degrees as our game progressed, but we continued with the stiff upper lip, for which the British are renowned. The golf finished with the scores level, so we organised an impromptu "skins" event, and we were just knuckling down to that challenge when wee David blurted out: "Oh boy, oh boy" – and promptly passed out from sunstroke. He had collapsed in a heap and was obviously struggling, so we took him back to the hotel, and told him to grab a few hours' sleep. He was looking really peaky and had turned lobster-pink, so, as the senior member in the Scotland ranks, I decided I would let him stay in bed and relax for the whole evening. However, by 6 p.m. he maintained that he had recovered, said there were no ill-effects and told me straight: "I am absolutely fine, there is no problem, so let's go out and have a party." There was just no stopping him.

'He was soon staggering around drunk as a lord, and barely capable of standing on his own. I glanced at the lad and thought to myself: "God, I wish I had persuaded him not to come." Then suddenly in walked Walter Smith with a grim look on his face, and he asked me: "Where's Speedie?" I was a bit flustered and mumbled: "Erm, he's just about to pass out on the couch over there, so there's no point trying to talk to him. He's plastered." At which point Smith, who was clearly furious, responded with all the affection of a speak-your-weight machine. "Right, this is a balls-up. You two were put in charge of him, and you had better get a grip of him, because he has been booked to appear live on *Grandstand* this evening. Take him back to the hotel, and sober him up smartish."

'Well, we were both flummoxed, but that was Walter. His attitude was that we had to accept personal responsibility for our actions: we were grown men, and we shouldn't have got ourselves in that mess in the first place. And he was right. The problem was that the BBC had requested an interview with David as part of their build-up to the second leg, and we had to do our best. So I took one of David's arms and Graeme held the other, and the pair of us dragged him to the studio link between Melbourne and London. By now he was babbling interminable nonsense, shouting: "How's it hangin', big man?" to strangers in the elevator, and I said to Sharp: "If we pull this off, it will be a miracle."

'Well, we didn't, and it wasn't. Bob Wilson [former Scotland goalkeeper turned sports anchorman] was on the line, and the plan was that he would lob a few easy questions over to Speedie. You have to remember that while it was around midday in Britain, it was really late on Saturday night in Melbourne. We tried to prop David up, between passing him orange juice and mineral water. But it was futile. He was sozzled. Eventually Bob began by asking: "Hello there, David, how are you enjoying yourself over there, and how is the Scottish squad acclimatising?" Whereupon our team-mate replied: "Ach, f***ing nae problem, big man, how's your-self?" At that moment, we heard the producer screaming into the microphone: "Get him off the f***ing line this instant!"

'And there was a brief announcement that the satellite had malfunctioned . . .'

The episode provided a rare note of levity in an otherwise insipid trip Down Under. Australia's coach Frank Arok had promised that the visitors would face a cauldron above and in front of them, but as it transpired Jim Leighton was in immaculate form in goals, and the match resulted in a no-scoring draw. Scotland, with their customary huffing and puffing, had reached their fourth consecutive World Cup finals, and the SFA swiftly confirmed that the Ferguson–Smith partnership would remain in charge for the 1986 campaign. What most people did not know was that the wheels were in motion for one of the most dramatic developments in Scottish football. After New Year, Smith began to hear murmurings of discontent from within Ibrox, where another league campaign had fallen flat with Rangers languishing far behind Hearts and eventual champions Celtic. Rangers started a process of restructuring with Lawrence Marlborough taking control and appointing David Holmes as his chairman. They searched for a high-profile figure with the clout to embark on a radical new policy for the organisation, and chose Graeme Souness, the Edinburgh-born firebrand who had starred at Liverpool and Sampdoria, and was a Scottish internationalist of repute. Holmes contacted Smith and they met at the Pond Hotel in Glasgow, where mutual admiration was palpable. The conversation touched on multifarious subjects without the question of money being broached. The next step was for Souness and Smith to sit down and discuss their respective ideas for the regeneration of Rangers to discover whether they could establish a viable partnership, and they met in the build-up to Scotland's friendly fixture with Romania, shortly before the World Cup finals. On the surface, they were starkly contrasting personalities. Souness was a well-heeled and well-groomed cosmopolitan character, who had even featured in a walk-on appearance in the television series *The Boys from the Black Stuff*, whereas Smith was an unassuming creature of habit with no airs and graces, who was rather akin to a Clydeside shop steward of yesteryear. Yet from the first moment of their encounter, Souness realised that he was in the presence of a true football man, and Smith recognised that his colleague-to-be harboured bold plans for Ibrox. The chemistry was right between the men and the die was cast, despite Jim McLean's reluctance to release his No. 2 from duties at Dundee United. When the news broke, he accused Rangers of poaching Smith, a charge which might have merited more serious consideration but for the dilatory fashion in which McLean had behaved three years earlier when presented with the opportunity to move to Ibrox. Even when Holmes submitted an official request to talk to Smith, and United agreed reluctantly to sanction the meeting, they refused to release their employee from his contract, and demanded significant compensation of £50,000. On this occasion Rangers refused to be dragged into any nonsense, and the energetic Holmes telephoned George Fox, asked the United director for an address to which he could dispatch the £50,000, wrote out the cheque in Smith's presence and summoned a courier. The cheque was delivered to Fox's Carnoustie residence that evening.

The subsequent period yielded a giddy whirl for Souness, Smith and for the institution that they had resolved to restore to glowing health. Stark evidence of the need for strong medicine in the wake of the regimes of Greig, and latterly Jock Wallace, was forthcoming when Smith finally fulfilled his boyhood dream by entering Ibrox as an employee in April 1986, aged 38. As he remembers, a swirl of thoughts enveloped his mind, and it would have been understandable had he indulged in some self-congratulation, but when the lifelong supporter signed his contract at Rangers, the team had just been defeated 2-1 by bottom-of-the-table Clydebank at Kilbowie. The torpid performance confirmed that too many of the senior personnel were inadequate. Nor were matters significantly better during the first game under Smith's oversight, when an industrious St Mirren beat Rangers at Love Street by the same score-line of 2-1. The prospect of European qualification seemed to be disappearing, particularly given that one of their two remaining matches was at Pittodrie, a venue which in recent times had developed into a northern fortress. 'The St Mirren defeat handed Graeme and I our first Ibrox crisis,' Smith reflects wryly. 'I'd been at the club less than a week, and Graeme hadn't even joined up yet!' Yet Smith's skills of organisation and motivation paid off when a Ted McMinn goal earned a 1-1 draw in Aberdeen, then Motherwell were defeated 2-0 with goals from Dave McPherson and Ally McCoist. Much of the play in these fixtures was unconvincing for fans accustomed to confident displays by their team, but at least the first objective of entry to Europe had been attained, albeit by a whisker.

Off the pitch, Smith was under no illusions. Indeed, the manner in which he trawled through the Ibrox corridors and surveyed the amenities and day-to-day running of the club merely emphasised the notion that glorious tradition alone does not guarantee continued success. On the pitch, the Rangers squad were long on perspiration, but painfully short of individuals to bring a spark of pizzazz to major European occasions. Though he ruled out snap judgments, his reports to Souness were couched in urgent terms, and the gauntlet was handed on to Holmes. There could be no quick solution without serious investment, and if that meant chasing major signings in England and Europe and breaking transfer records, there was no alternative.

Smith and Souness had been provided with an opportunity to engage in some detailed planning, but sadly such conditions were scarcely available for Scotland's World Cup campaign in Mexico, where a low-key exit followed a lacklustre tournament for Alex Ferguson's men. According to reports from several of the squad, the team were riven with factions with Ferguson and Souness constantly at odds, when Scottish fans might have assumed that the priority was tackling Denmark, West Germany and Uruguay. It was suggested by some that the explanation for the breakdown in the relationship was that Ferguson had coveted the Rangers job, which is implausible when it is recalled that he had knocked it back in 1983, and anyway he was poised to decamp to take charge of Manchester United. Whatever the reason for the schism, Smith had to use all his diplomatic skills to keep the channels of communication open. Alan Rough, a non-playing member of the squad on this occasion, again provides telling insight on squabbling that he witnessed:

'The SFA had decided that Scotland players should only be permitted one three-minute telephone call home twice a week, which was pretty pathetic for those guys with wives and young children, especially when you considered the wads of cash which were swilling around in the governing body's coffers. Well, as soon as he heard about the phone restrictions, Graeme Souness went ballistic and told the rest of us: "This is f***ing ridiculous," and elected to fight our corner. It developed into a really big argument between him and Alex with the pair bawling at each other, but that wasn't out of the ordinary in Mexico. On the contrary, at nearly every meeting the players held with Alex – and Graeme was the head of the players' committee, so there were plenty – they seemed to become embroiled in shouting matches, frequently over the most trivial of matters, and it was hardly conducive to fostering a climate of unity. To be fair, Walter did his best to act as mediator, but since everybody knew he was linking up at Rangers with Graeme as soon as the World Cup was over, that hardly improved the atmosphere.'

Internal divisions had emerged prior to the tournament, when Souness and a group of the perceived party animals within the Scotland ensemble, including Frank McAvennie, Mo Johnston and Graeme Sharp, drove into Los Angeles in a chauffeur-driven limousine for a meal with Rod Stewart, at the superstar's behest, and dined on oysters, caviare and champagne at a plush restaurant on Sunset Boulevard. For Ferguson, who had nurtured his outstanding Aberdeen side on the virtues of temperance and staying out of the limelight away from football, this was the kind of reckless behaviour which might have been specifically designed to attract hordes of paparazzi. Smith, while hardly lax on the disciplinary front, looked far more benevolently upon the players' soirée with Stewart: after all, the singer acted as an unofficial ambassador for the Tartan Army. This should not be misinterpreted as suggesting that Ferguson and Smith were involved in some sort of petty stand-off, but the focus of both men, and Souness too, seemed to be a few thousand miles away. An illustration of this comes in a conversation with Rough, in which Souness outlined the magnitude of vision for his forthcoming role at Rangers. Rough remembers:

'We shared a couple of beers outside his hotel room, and he spoke of how David Holmes was prepared to bankroll a revolution at Ibrox by recruiting some genuinely international-class performers. I was sceptical at first, and inquired: "Who exactly are we talking about here?" Then calm as you please, Souness replied: "Well, I have been studying all the good sides in recent years, and their success has been based round a spine of a top-notch keeper, an inspirational centre-half, a midfield supremo and a prolific striker, and that is why I am doing my best to bring people of the calibre of Chris Woods, Terry Butcher and Trevor Steven to Glasgow. What we need is a total transformation of Scottish football, and if Rangers are ever to become a truly leading European club, we have to broaden our horizons and change our attitude to everything from diet and nutrition to creating soccer academies and introducing the kids to good habits." It was strong stuff, and I have to admit that while I believe the subsequent influx of foreign players has been detrimental to Scottish football, Souness was a genuine visionary, and his arguments made a lot of sense.'

Given this backdrop, the Scots' World Cup road meandered to nowhere in Mexico. They lost 1-0 to the Danes, courtesy of Preben Elkjaer-Larsen's 58th-minute goal, then succumbed 2-1 to the Germans, Rudi Voller cancelling out Gordon Strachan's excellent early strike before Klaus Allofs secured a deserved victory. Controversy subsequently surfaced when Ferguson dropped Souness from the squad for the final match against Uruguay, which still offered a chance of progression to the later stages. It was a baffling selection from the usually astute Ferguson, with Paul McStay introduced to the fray for the first time in the competition with Arthur Albiston, Paul Sturrock and, to his immense surprise, Graeme Sharp. The line was peddled by the management that Souness was suffering from dehydration after his notable industry in the defeat by the Germans, but few within the camp believed this, and it was impossible to avoid the suspicion that his omission was due to a personality clash. For his part, Smith was in constant contact with Souness as they made a string of international calls to a raft of potential Rangers signings. Ferguson, no stranger to banner headlines, declined to comment on the ditching of Souness, apart from sticking to the party line. Some players, who were bored to distraction in their sub-standard accommodation, actually began to wonder whether elimination might not be preferable to being asked to tackle a rampaging Argentina team in the quarter-finals, and it was scarcely a surprise when the Scots served up one of their most innocuous performances in slipping to a goal-less draw versus Uruguay, whose Jose Batista was sent off in the first minute of the proceedings for a horrible challenge on Strachan. Even with a long-term numerical advantage, Ferguson's men barely engineered a clear-cut opening as the Uruguayans put up the shutters. The Tartan Army barely had the strength to vent their disapproval in the heat that engulfed them.

❖

At this point speculation over Souness and Smith's impact on Rangers was rewarded with some genuine news, and if any of the ranks of Ibrox fans had been sceptical over some of the names linked with their club, the events of the summer of 1986 countered their misgivings to a large extent. The imposing Terry Butcher joined on 1 August and Chris Woods, the sort of high-class goalkeeper that the club had required for years, also began looking at plots of land in the Dunblane area, clearly convinced that he was destined for a lengthy stay in Scotland. Souness laid out his vision to a reverential media, and it was evident that substance matched the hype. He had been appointed as Rangers' player-manager, though, and he had no experience of coaching at any level, which meant that Smith's role was crucial. As Butcher explains, he rose to the challenge superbly well:

'Walter was very knowledgeable about tactics and what makes people tick, and we had some great times at Rangers between 1986 and 1990. My quote when he was eventually installed in the Scotland job [in 2004] was that he was a great manager, because he likes heavy-metal music and red wine – a couple of assets that any decent manager should possess. But being serious, Walter was the one who organised things like set-pieces, and he would walk and talk things through with you, like who you were up against and what their qualities were. He was a different character to Graeme: more methodical, more technical, more interested in hard graft than pretty stuff, and that made him a perfect foil for Souness. He had a terrific manner about him, an aura which inspired confidence, and if anybody can promote a feel-good factor, and get the best from players, it is him.'

Rangers' supporters realised soon enough that while Souness would command centre-stage and doubtless generate lashings of trenchant raw material for sports journalists, Smith was every bit as significant to the club's future. Long-term supporter and author Alex Anderson provides this interpretation:

'A man who cut as measured and modest a public figure as Souness appeared glamorous and confrontational, Smith was a quietly hard man, whose calm demeanour was wrought from steel. Though no one would have guessed it from his on-camera persona, Walter was not averse to inviting training-ground mutineers into the privacy of the dressing room, locking the door and offering them the first punch. He was the studied personality who had studied the Scottish football scene his entire life. Alex Totten and John Hagart departed Ibrox along with Jock Wallace, and Smith was a change in the right direction in terms of coaching staff. However, mere change was not enough to retrieve Rangers from the embarrassment they had become to the heavyweights of British football they would soon be: what was required was a tectonic shift. That could only manifest itself through a singularly chaotic, destructive force of nature. Smith was, if you like, the method behind the Souness madness.'

As the Souness era commenced, some predicted grimly that he would eventually bankrupt Scottish football. What should not be forgotten, though, is that Butcher and Woods, respectively the England captain and the deputy goalkeeper to Peter Shilton, cost the club £1.2m which, seen from a distance, seems like the bargain of the century. And despite the further recruitment of striker Colin West, David Holmes was not endowed with the financial resources which David Murray would bring to Rangers upon his arrival in 1988. Once the two English players had staked their future at Ibrox, no more money was available in the transfer market, as Smith publicly confirmed. 'We were told that we could not afford to bring in another class player. Although we were to spend far more money in the years ahead, we had reached our limit with these first signings. That was why it was so important to Graeme and me, as well as to the club, that the signings we made were the right signings, and it turned out they were the men for the job.' No immediate indication of a glorious renaissance was in evidence, though, when Rangers commenced their Scottish league campaign against Hibs at Easter Road. Quite the contrary, because Souness marked his playing debut for Rangers by scything into opposing centre-forward George McCluskey, and he was red-carded. That precipitated a mass brawl, though Hibs' goalkeeper Alan Rough was not involved. He had been booked, and did not wish to risk joining Souness in the dressing room. Butcher describes the match and the follow-up:

> 'It was neither the best of sights, nor the best of starts: Ally McCoist scored from the penalty spot, but we lost 2-1. I ended up getting a yellow card in my first game, and afterwards the SFA decreed that everybody who was involved in the fracas would receive two penalty points, so with my other booking I managed to pick up four disciplinary points on my league debut. A nice quiet start to life in Scotland. After the match, Souness was a nightmare. We went out in Edinburgh that evening to drown our sorrows, but he almost finished up in a fight in a bar. A guy was trying to be smart and clever and I tried to placate him, but Graeme got fed up with his attitude and told him to f*** off. It was time to catch a taxi back to the Norton House Hotel, and some sort of sanity, before something worse happened to cloud a pretty bad day.'

Butcher's testimony explains why Walter Smith had to navigate through choppy waters on many occasions. At his best, Souness was a dominant, wonderfully aggressive threat to any opponents, blessed with skill, vision and an instinct which had been refined at Liverpool. On the debit side, he had a long history of lunging into wild challenges when the red mist descended, and in these instances he was often a liability to those around him. At these moments, it was incumbent on Smith to dictate matters from the sidelines, and almost to ignore his nominal boss. Treading this tightrope requires calmness and tact, but Smith had learned the balancing act in his association with Jim McLean, who also tended to operate on a short fuse. A member of the team that lost to Hibs that day reveals: 'He didn't make a big fuss about it, but Walter was worried that there might be a breakdown in communication because of Graeme's decision to play on. And you have to believe it: there were tensions and a lot of pressure on both men in the build-up to that match, and the worst possible thing that could have happened did happen, with Souness losing the plot. But I spoke to Walter at the end, and he said to me: "Better it all goes off today than later in the season." He couldn't have been more in check of his emotions, and he was more disappointed with the result than the fight. It tells you something about the guy. Yes, he's a decent bloke, but he is as tough as old boots.'

That was just as well, because there was no disguising the fact that, in the early stages of the season, Rangers were still punching below their weight. The Hibs reverse might have been shrugged off, but when Souness's men toiled to beat Falkirk at Ibrox in their next match and then surrendered a two-goal half-time lead at the same venue in losing 3-2 to Dundee United, they were languishing in seventh place in the championship table, and anxious followers sensed that something was amiss. The pre-match regimen which had been introduced by Souness was one of the most obvious sources of discontent, since the new manager, who was deter-mined to do things his way, had decreed that the players would train on Friday mornings, then spend the next 24 hours at the Grosvenor Hotel in Glasgow. Alas, most of the young men who had been dragged away from families and friends in a futile attempt at team-building, were bored witless. A sound rationale, no doubt, lurked behind the ploy by Souness, which may have worked in Italy where Serie A clubs can be separated by long distances, but it seemed absurd for players to be shunted off to the confines of a hotel when they were due to face Falkirk, Hamilton or Celtic the following afternoon. Soon enough, after Butcher and McCoist had broached the subject with Walter Smith, he persuaded his colleague to ring the changes, and he duly obliged. It was not the only time that diplomatic intervention would be required to ensure that the managerial partnership flourished.

Rangers began building momentum as August progressed, and the process was helped greatly by the first Old Firm match of season 1986–87, played at Ibrox. For Smith, who had grown up to relish these occasions, this was the first significant test of his qualities and capabilities, and he admitted later that it was one of the most memorable afternoons of his life. To be sure, it was a fairly humdrum encounter enlivened only by a trademark spark of genius from Davie Cooper, whose reverse pass pierced the Celtic defence and allowed Ian Durrant to whack the ball past Pat Bonnar. But when that goal was scored a crescendo of noise enveloped the ground, as fans who had been starved of success for too long rejoiced. Smith and every person associated with the club were treated to a huge surge of adrenaline, and lingering apprehension that this was another false dawn ebbed away as Rangers produced an impressive sequence of six victories in their next eight fixtures to start climbing the league table.

As successes were chalked up, the mood was transformed not merely within the club's support, but among those who worked for the organisation, as one former employee told me, with an Anglo-Saxon flourish:

'By the mid-1980s, we had reached the stage of thinking that we might have to dwell on the glories of the past. Some of my mates had even stopped going to matches, preferring to spend their time at junior games on Saturday, where they didn't have to listen to anybody talking about Celtic or f***ing Aberdeen. That was one of the key areas where Souness made a difference: he walked in the door big and strong and proud, and obviously didn't give a f*** what anybody else thought, and told the board: "Right, you used to do things this way, but now you are going to do it my way." When you look back at what Graeme actually did, it wasn't rocket science. I mean, why on earth Rangers hadn't been interested in players such as Butcher and Woods before he arrived was a mystery to me. Let's face it, if you go to clubs like Coventry and Norwich and tell world-class players: "Here's the chance to play in front of 50,000 supporters on a regular basis, as well as a higher profile than you will ever get in England," why wouldn't they want to come to Scotland? Especially if you remember that the English clubs were banned from European competition [after the fatal rioting at the 1985 European Cup final at Heysel]. But Souness was a showman, and he lifted up our spirits in the space of a few weeks. Even when he was doing mental things like getting sent off at Hibs, it just showed he was never going to take a backward step.'

That belief intensified on 27 October when Souness and Smith collected their first item of silverware after Rangers defeated Celtic 2-1 in the Skol Cup final, goals from Ian Durrant and Davie Cooper sealing a significant triumph for the club. The result was a testimony to the new-found confidence which the management team had instilled in their players, and the afternoon demonstrated the bond that had been forged between the duo and the mercurial Cooper, who was destined to become one of the tragic figures of Scottish football. For years, the elusive and instinctively unpredictable winger had danced to his own tune, transcending the mediocrity of many around him, which justified the assertion of Dutch master Ruud Gullit that he was the best player he had come up against. With Souness in charge, Coop was allowed licence to parade his panache with an increasingly gifted squad. Throughout his career, Cooper had suffered, somewhat like Kenny Dalglish, from possessing too much vision. He would, for instance, dispatch a glorious 50-yard pass, only to be let down by the failure of a team mate to capitalise on the situation. But his talents were certainly appreciated by Souness: 'Coop was special'; by Butcher: 'One of the best I have ever played with', and by Smith: 'Coop could have featured in any team you care to name. He was a magnificent footballer.' As Rangers battled their way to glory in the League Cup, their strengths were greatly admired by the watching Graham Roberts and Chris Waddle, who spoke later about the fantastic atmosphere which the game had generated. It was not long before Roberts, a fractious and aggressive individual who provided a fearful prospect for rival strikers, was signing on the dotted line and pledging his future to a club which, up to 1986, had been in danger of slipping into a sad state of disrepair. It is simplistic to downgrade the Souness achievements with the rejoinder that he has not achieved anything in football without recourse to investment in lavish signings, but so far as Smith was concerned, this was the start of a beautiful friendship, his view expressed succinctly:

> 'He was the catalyst for change. He turned the dream into reality. He brought it alive. Without him, it wouldn't have happened. He knew these players; they knew him. And they recognised that if Graeme Souness was going to continue his career in Scotland, then it was worthwhile joining him.'

By the end of the year, Rangers were on the march once more. They had beaten Celtic in their two most recent meetings, had collected a trophy for a fan base long starved of reasons to be cheerful, and had sailed into the UEFA Cup with an assurance which suggested that Souness's knowledge of European football might be invaluable in the years ahead. The campaign commenced with a potentially fraught tussle against Finnish club Ilves Tampere, but Cooper, who was ubiquitous during this period, was in sublime form in the first leg at Ibrox, and helped to orchestrate a 4-0 win. Robert Fleck scored a hat-trick, and Ally McCoist applied the *coup de grâce*. It was game, set and match, which was just as well, for in the return leg – without the services of Souness, who was injured, Ted McMinn and Derek Ferguson – Rangers were ragged and unconvincing in slipping to a 2-0 defeat with goals from Aro Hjelm and Arto Uimonen. Souness, watching from the sidelines with his usual saturnine stare, declared: 'We played like a pub team.' Progress had been secured and embarrassment averted nonetheless, and in the next round Rangers were paired with Boavista of Portugal. This proved to be a more daunting task, as expected, and the Ibrox support were stunned when Toninho broke the deadlock on the half-hour. Dave

McPherson levelled matters within three minutes, and as half-time beckoned Butcher fed the ball to McCoist, and the prolific striker finished the attack decisively. It was a narrow advantage, particularly considering that the Scots had conceded an away goal, but Smith checked out Boavista at home, and he and Souness retained the faith that their personnel would secure the tie. This they did with a display which was as professional and masterful as their second outing against Ilves Tampere had been shoddy. Thanks to a nerveless display from Woods, the hosts grew increasingly desperate, and Derek Ferguson was the beneficiary of Cooper's inch-perfect lay-off, scoring the solitary goal in the 70th minute. It sparked feverish celebrations from the band of travelling fans, for this was the first instance that Rangers had advanced to round three since the giddy success in Barcelona 14 years previously.

Few were deluded into proclaiming that Rangers were now capable of troubling the super-heavyweights of the European scene, certainly no one from the Souness-Smith school of pragmatic assessment, or any supporter who examined the playing squad and noticed individuals such as Bobby Russell, Jimmy Nicholl, Cammy Fraser and Stuart Munro still commanding regular slots. By the stage of their third-round meeting with Borussia Moenchengladbach in late November and early December, Rangers were in the process of signing Roberts from Tottenham Hotspur for £450,000 – which proved to be another outstanding piece of business – but he would obviously have no part to play in what developed into an old-fashioned scrap between two fiercely committed teams. The Scots had the opportunity to build an advantage, but despite thrilling their fans with an early goal from McCoist following a superbly constructed build-up, they created a string of excellent chances only to be punished with a sucker-punch equaliser after 30 minutes when Uwe Rahn latched on to Andre Winkhold's cross, and headed past Woods. That was it at Ibrox, but Rangers had triumphed abroad on their previous mission, and remained positive for the re-match in Germany. They had good reason to feel they were well in contention, given the belligerence with which they roared into action at the Bokelborg Stadion, but McCoist struck the bar, Butcher was denied a stonewall penalty, and as the match raged on the Germans seemed content to cling on for a goalless draw. Rangers suffered another blow when Munro was dismissed after a clash with Winkhold. It would have demoralised most sides, but the visitors were unstinting in their labours, eventually to no avail. In what seemed an absurd conclusion, Cooper was booked for comments made as he was poised to take a free-kick in the 87th minute. Referee Alex Ponnet suddenly remembered that he had already cautioned the player, hence a red card for a second Rangers player.

This occasion perhaps could be regarded as a microcosm of Rangers in Europe under Graeme Souness. There was no shortage of passion, tenacity or craft, but too often the essential touch of class would emerge from rivals, or they would find themselves the victims of botched officialdom. By the death, as Borussia clung on for a scarcely merited draw, Butcher was in tears, though the big fellow and his comrades paid tribute to the 3,500 supporters who had followed them to the Continent. It would be no consolation that Moenchengladbach were knocked out in the semi-finals of the tournament 2-0 on aggregate . . . by Dundee United.

CHAPTER FIVE

TROPHIES, TRIALS AND TRIBULATIONS

❖

'The guilty pair shook their heads in disbelief'

When one considers Rangers' experiences under Graeme Souness and Walter Smith during 1987 and '88, it is possible to detect a battle between benign and malign influences for the soul of the club, the occasional lurch into insanity and the regular straining of the credulity of thousands of fans. Freak results were in the mix, too.

Hence a team packed with superstars were knocked out of the Scottish Cup by Hamilton Academical months after many of the same players had performed wonders in beating the mighty Dynamo Kiev, and an eruption of violence during an Old Firm tussle led to Terry Butcher being vilified by the tabloids, one infamous headline proclaiming: 'Goldilocks and the Three Bears', a description which is explained later in the chapter. Then there was the puzzling case of Robert Fleck.

Early in the new regime at Ibrox, Souness had decided, in the no-nonsense style which made him unpopular with some sections of the Scottish public, that Fleck was not up to the standards he required in skill or keeping his discipline, which some thought a bit rich coming from a fiery character such as the manager. He and Walter Smith discussed the matter, and concluded that the player would be better off leaving. Smith phoned his mate Jocky Scott, who was in charge of Dundee FC at that point and urgently required a striker. Scott told Smith that he would be interested in acquiring Fleck, but that the cash-flow situation was desperate. Smith returned to Souness with this information, and they agreed to reduce the player's transfer to £20,000 – this for a footballer who subsequently won four Scotland caps – but even that asking price was still too much, and the prospective deal fell through. Yet, within months of Fleck languishing in the reserves, he bounced back into contention with a series of fine performances for Rangers' senior team. Lo and behold, Norwich were sufficiently impressed to make a bid for him, amounting to £580,000, which led to his moving to Carrow Road, and eventually to Chelsea for the sum of £2.1m.

Thus as 1987 appeared on the horizon, the suspicion was that Souness's Jekyll-and-Hyde personality would leave his players and supporters wondering on a regular basis whether they stood on the verge of a windfall or a catastrophe. In the Ne'erday Old Firm clash came resounding affirmation of how Celtic's grip on their title was being loosened, but even here life could have been so different for player/manager Souness. He piled into the Celtic captain Roy Aitken early in the game with a cynical challenge which earned him a yellow card, but also had the effect of knocking the stuffing out of his opponent for the rest of the encounter. Had the card been red, Souness would have had no excuse, but his ploy worked as McCoist and Fleck established a comfortable cushion for the hosts, and that proved the catalyst for Souness to taunt the opposition with a succession of back-heels and flicks, as if emphasising his team's superiority over the old enemy. The Edinburgh man had clearly decided that he could not care less whether Celtic's support burned effigies of him later: he had laid down the battle lines and issued a resounding declaration of intent. Which is fine, until fate intervenes.

Rangers entertained lowly Hamilton on 31 January reflecting the sort of arrogance which comes from those who anticipate a mis-match, though this was the 20th anniversary of their notorious exit in the cup competition at the hands of unsung Berwick

Rangers. On paper it should have been a rout, but Scottish Cup ties offer no guarantees, and after Adrian Sprott had sent the underdogs in front, the 1,200–1,500 Hamilton fans basked in what they assumed was to be a brief spell in the spotlight. Gerry Collins almost made it 2-0, however, and the likes of Souness and Roberts were clearly discomfited by the lung-bursting efforts of their rivals. Rangers mounted a sustained onslaught, but Hamilton's defence held firm, thanks to a rash of frantic goal-line clearances and desperate hacks to safety, while the crowd grew ever more hostile towards the wee team. Robert Paterson was one of the visiting supporters who savoured the cup shock, but his recollections demonstrate some of the more noisome aspects of Rangers during the Souness era:

'It was a great day, but it was also pretty scary. When we got to the ground, as usual wearing our scarves, there was the usual patronising stuff from their fans, asking us to enjoy life in a big stadium, because it would be the only thing we enjoyed that afternoon. You can cope with that, it comes with the territory, but once the game started and Sprotty scored, it was as if we had broken some law or other. There was this old guy in an expensive suit and tie – he looked as if he might be an accountant or a lawyer – but he was hurling this non-stop stream of sectarian abuse at the guys in the Hamilton team, who he regarded as being Catholics, and it was just sickening listening to this endless torrent of F words and C words; and the C didn't stand for Catholic, by the way. In the final 20 minutes, somebody flung a few coins at me, and I was advised by a couple of stewards to take off my scarf "for yer ain health". But what the hell was that about?

'Then, when I walked out of the stadium at the end, a group of the more inebriated Rangers fans milled around me and my mate and began pushing and shoving us, hoping we would retaliate and get in a ruck. We didn't respond, so they eventually started calling us "f***ing poofs" and other such insults, and that went on for the best part of 10 or 15 minutes. And the worst thing was that a couple of Strathclyde Police officers were only standing a few yards away from us, and they never batted an eyelid, almost as if they were saying to the Rangers guys: "Go on, tell them to f*** off. That's what they deserve for knocking the mighty Rangers out of the cup."

'Put it like this: we were happy to get back to Hamilton, but that episode showed me that Rangers were developing this mentality again, where you weren't allowed to beat them. They had kind of lost that during the previous decade, because they were pretty crap and Aberdeen and Dundee United had climbed above them, but when Souness came to Ibrox, he had clearly got the message rammed home that they needed a siege mentality. "Nobody likes us, and we don't care" . . . that sort of thing, which was a bit pathetic. I'm not saying they should have cheered our victory, but would it really have hurt them to have let us enjoy one of our best-ever results?'

The short answer, from the perspective of Souness and Smith, was a resounding yes. For them, embarking on a crusade which had to be swift and brutal, there was simply no room for sentiment, particularly in light of the manner in which chief executive Holmes had irritated sections of the Rangers support by his apparent lack of interest in helping them cheer on their heroes while in European action. Club historian Robert McElroy commented: 'The relatively small number of Light Blue followers who wanted to travel to Finland [for the Ilves Tampere game] found their best efforts obstructed by the club, with chief executive David Holmes and his sidekick, the former Mars Bar salesman Freddie Fletcher, regarding supporters as an intrusion and an encumbrance rather than customers.' It was a volatile period in football in general, but an exaggerated tension afflicted Ibrox which Smith, as courteous and civilised as he was, could not ease, and certainly not as Souness's men powered their way towards the championship with a philosophy that owed more to industry than inspiration. Nor did the ceaseless niggle do anything to dissuade sceptics that Souness's grand plan basically amounted to assembling a squad that reflected his bombastic and bullying approach, and to hell with outdated notions of the beautiful game. When Rangers were finally beaten by Celtic towards the end of the season, by 3-1 at Parkhead, even the likes of Butcher, newly recruited to the Ibrox scene, got caught up in the sectarian strife: he reacted to the green walls and Celtic crest in the bathroom by taking a couple of pictures of the Queen into the Rangers dressing room and placing them at each end. Butcher, who is an intelligent man and who has since become involved with the anti-bigotry group Nil By Mouth, seems mystified nowadays about how he could have been captivated by factors that he did not fully understand. But if there was a serious sectarian problem, few were intent on facing up to it in 1987.

After victories over Dundee, Clydebank and Hearts, Rangers journeyed to Aberdeen on 2 May with a chance of securing the title, but only if Celtic came unstuck against Falkirk. It was another in the list of controversial occasions for Souness, who was given a torrid time by the home side's sprightly Brian Irvine, before responding with a nasty challenge, which earned him another red card. As for the match itself, Butcher opened the scoring when he latched on to a Cooper free-kick, only for Irvine to equalise at the end of the first half. It was fraught and frenetic with too many fouls and not enough football, but Butcher and Roberts mopped up the pressure, and news filtered through to the players that Celtic had lost. And so, with Pittodrie festooned in red, white and blue, the Souness era had seized significant spoils – with the ultimate assistance of Celtic. For Smith, there was satisfaction that his club had won their first league title for nine seasons, but certainly no triumphalism on his part, given that he recognised as much as anybody that their success had been only fitfully convincing, and that greater challenges lay ahead. However, having been involved in the capture of two trophies after such a barren spell for Rangers, Smith knew that at least the management had the fans on their side for the foreseeable future, an important factor considering the intrinsic fickleness of Ibrox supporters en masse.

In some respects, the months ahead proved frustrating for the Souness/Smith duopoly. Football writers fuelled speculation that a string of high-profile signings, on a level with Butcher and Woods, were poised to put pen to paper, but frequently such tales were inspired by chit-chat in the pub or in the confines of a supporters' club, such is the fashion in which rumours and reality become intertwined in Glasgow gossip about the Old Firm. In the event, once some of the more fanciful notions had been laid to rest, Souness had to settle for a bargain-basement collection, recruiting Avi Cohen, a former team-mate at Liverpool, Trevor Francis, an old colleague at Sampdoria, and Watford's Marc Falco. These were hard-working professionals, especially Francis, but not the dynamic young talents that the club required, particularly since Souness was winding down his long and impressive playing career, and was becoming increasingly prone to injury and provoking the wrath of referees for mistimed tackles. Unsurprisingly, he perceived the latter phenomenon as a conspiracy, and if one trait epitomised the Souness years with Rangers, it was conflict. Officialdom, rival managers, the press and broadcasters were regularly at loggerheads with the temperamental Scot, and while his outbursts provided rich fare for red-top papers in particular, they merely acted as fodder for those who held grievances against Rangers. Perhaps Souness enjoyed the incessant spats. Few others did.

Back in the engine-room, where Smith was in his element, the club prepared for the 1987–88 campaign, and the No. 2 sensed that this would present a far stiffer test than their maiden season. Celtic were heading into their centenary year, and there was a renewed frisson of purpose and solidarity in their camp, even if the biscuit-tin approach to buying and selling had left their resources looking limited. Though the performances of Terry Butcher since his induction to Scottish football had been typically industrious, he was such a wholehearted warrior that there was always the risk he might incur a serious injury. In the midst of a fractious meeting with Aberdeen at Ibrox in November, that scenario materialised, the big Englishman suffering a leg break after a collision with Alex McLeish, which forced him to accept that he would play no further part in the renewed championship bid. Before that blow, Souness could afford a brief spell of basking in glory when Dynamo Kiev, opponents of high quality, were beaten over two nerve-shredding European Cup encounters in September, not least because at the Republic Stadium his team produced a resilient and controlled display in front of 100,000 spectators. Though Rangers eventually conceded a goal after 72 minutes, when Alexei Mikhailichenko converted a penalty award, they and their band of supporters, who had braved labyrinths of red tape in fulfilling travel plans, returned to Scotland with the feeling that the tie was there to be won. Such thoughts were justified, but not without ritual controversy. When the Soviet champions trained in Glasgow on the night before the return leg, they readied themselves for battle on a normal-sized Ibrox pitch. However, 24 hours later, at the behest of Souness, the touchlines had been narrowed on both wings in a bid to negate the width and pace of Kiev's skilful wingers Vasily Rats and Oleg Blokhin. Whether this was within the spirit of the game was debatable, but the legality of Rangers' actions was not in question according to the UEFA regulations. The ploy certainly unsettled the Russians to the extent that they gifted their adversaries the lead with a howler from goalkeeper Victor Chanov, whose abortive clearance struck Sergei Baltacha on the backside, teeing the ball up for Ally McCoist, who fed on to Falco to score in the 25th minute. On such nights, with the Ibrox throng in full voice, the stadium can resemble a revivalist meeting, and as the din swelled with Rangers controlling most of the play, a Francis cross was headed on by Falco to McCoist, who guided the ball into the corner of the net. Kiev flung everything they could muster at their hosts for the last half-hour, a period which seemed to drag on, and on, but there was to be no denying Souness's team a famous victory. He rushed out towards his side, and one might have imagined that they had won the cup itself. Not too many occasions in the months ahead would link the words smile and Souness.

❖

The events of 17 October 1987 and thereafter seem almost farcical when viewed from this distance. Celtic, who were desperate to restore their winning ways, had signed the redoubtable trio of Andy Walker, Frank McAvennie and Mick McCarthy, and after losing the season's first Old Firm tussle by 2-0, despite Souness being sent off yet again, they recognised that they could not afford any more slip-ups. Consequently, when Rangers and Celtic next met in the league, on a bad-natured afternoon, strewn with petty vindictiveness, the Ibrox men lost the plot in spectacular fashion. McAvennie crashed into Chris Woods on three occasions in the early stages, bundling him into his net on the second and boxing his ears on the third. Woods grabbed his assailant round the throat with one hand, McAvennie sought to slap him away, then Butcher charged over and pushed his opponent in the chest. Graham Roberts was next into the frame, contact was made between him and the Celtic striker, who collapsed in a heap. The referee produced red cards for Woods and McAvennie, but if official sanctions were meant to restore relative calm, they failed dismally. Butcher then scored an embarrassing own-goal, lofting the ball over stand-in keeper Roberts as Celtic established a 2-0 interval advantage. When the action resumed, Butcher next became involved in a collision with rival goalkeeper Alan McKnight, aimed a little kick at the Celtic man, and was promptly shown a second yellow, and a red card. As he sat in the Ibrox dressing room disconsolately, McCoist and Richard Gough managed to salvage a 2-2 draw for their team in the unlikeliest of circumstances, but for all the headlines that this encounter provoked, they were as nothing to the mounting resentment which was accruing against Rangers, for their alleged over-physicality.

In this respect Souness and Smith were as one. Earlier in the

1980s, Rangers' line-ups had started to look frail when placed under pressure, and Alex Ferguson's Aberdeen had grown renowned for successfully challenging their hated Glasgow rivals. For a club who had long prided themselves on never contemplating a backward step, this was humiliating, and the new management determined that they would not countenance fielding any individual who was not prepared to respond to muscle with more of the same. 'All I ask of my players is that they offer me 100 per cent, and walk off the pitch feeling as if they have nothing more to give,' said Smith. 'If somebody gets stuck in and chases the ball endlessly, I shouldn't criticise him for that, I should be thankful that he is bothered enough to get involved. What do you want me to do: look for guys who aren't bothered, people who don't care?' While one can understand Smith's reasoning, there is a certain naivety in his argument, if for no other reason than that the team were under increasing scrutiny as the 1980s unfolded. Butcher, for instance, was asked to report to Govan police station after the acrimonious Old Firm tussle, and he was joined by Rangers' operations officer Alistair Hood and solicitor Len Murray, as a prelude to being informed that he was being charged with behaviour likely to cause a breach of the peace. This struck him like a bolt from the blue, and the affair attracted wide press coverage and many conspiracy theories on football phone-in programmes, before it emerged that Butcher, Woods, Roberts and McAvennie were all facing charges. Despite some sporting observers deploying the facile argument that the courts were no place for footballers' misdeamours, a trial date was fixed for 12 April 1988.

Readers should understand the culture of mutual loathing that existed between the two sides of the Old Firm divide at that time. McAvennie, a character who was later lampooned as a leering Lothario intent on merry-making with the nearest maiden in TV programmes such as *Only an Excuse*, was actually a rumbustious player who was well acquainted in the dark arts of soccer. Roberts, by comparison, was a surly individual whose life has not been short of unsavoury scraps, while Woods and Butcher were among English footballers who were not simply sucked into the Old Firm vortex when they signed for Rangers, but seemed to feel that they had to behave even worse than the Scots on the pitch, as if to justify their inflated salaries. None of this should be regarded as a vindication of what materialised at Ibrox on that mad October day, but having examined all the relevant evidence, the outcome of the proceedings at Glasgow Sheriff Court still strikes me as incomprehensible. The four accused, who had been dubbed 'Goldilocks and the Three Bears' in tabloid style, sat together, but none of the Rangers trio spoke a word to McAvennie, who was regarded by them as the agent provocateur, which he was. Evidence was presented about crowd incitement and the referee's report was discussed at length, and as the trial progressed it appeared that the outcome would be nothing more serious than judicial slaps on the wrist for the footballers. Such predictions proved ill-founded. McAvennie was found not guilty; Roberts breathed a sigh of relief when the case against him was found not proven; Butcher was pronounced guilty and fined £250; Woods was also convicted, but a £500 fine was imposed. The guilty pair shook their heads in disbelief. Even at this juncture, Butcher claims that he cannot fathom the thought processes behind that week spent in court, though he clearly believes that the trial was whipped up by political expediency, and that it had less to do with the Scottish justice system than government posturing. His view:

'Prime Minister Margaret Thatcher hated football, hated its re-putation, and loathed the way that its hooligans had tarnished Britain's image abroad. This was only three years after the Heysel tragedy, remember, and English clubs were still banned from Europe. And to this day I have a strong feeling that Woodsy and me, as high-profile players, were used as an example. Just consider the events on the pitch at Easter Road during my first league game for Rangers [when Souness was sent off for the George

McCluskey challenge] . . . that was much more likely, I would have thought, to cause a riot than the brief flashpoint in what was, after all, an Old Firm derby. What would they have done in a similar political climate after the more recent Manchester United and Arsenal melees? Put them away for life? I had done worse things on a football pitch, and not found myself standing in court. So why did it happen this time?'

Twenty years on, such an incident might be dismissed as another storm in the pint glass of Scottish football, but it heightened the perception that the two Glasgow institutions were being treated in contrasting fashions. As the perpetrator, 'Goldilocks' McAvennie should have suffered at least the fate as his two Rangers counterparts, but the disparity in verdicts simply reinforced the suspicion, prevalent at Ibrox that everybody was against the Bears, even the judiciary and the police. Celtic, by comparison, were constantly depicted as downtrodden victims who benefited from a saccharine media spin, which allowed them to present themselves as good-natured jesters who were interested only in aesthetic football, while the much-reviled 'Huns' were miserable Calvinists on the hunt for a scrap. It should be added that much of the rampant paranoia at both clubs was a by-product of sad little conspiracy theorists, but the tensions boiled over with increasing regularity on Souness's watch. Smith, a more insightful customer by comparison, is notable for resembling the dog in the Sherlock Holmes story *Silver Blaze*. He didn't bark.

❖

With Butcher out injured, Richard Gough returned from Tottenham Hotspur, but there was no doubt that Rangers stuttered badly in that second season. They retained the Scottish League Cup in a pulsating final with Aberdeen, the match finishing 3-3 and being settled by a 5-3 advantage in the penalty shoot-out. They beat Dynamo Kiev, a meritorious achievement, and they eliminated the Poles of Gornik Zabrze 4-2 on aggregate in the next round, McCoist once more to the fore with a brace of goals, one in each leg. But reality could not be ignored. 'Basically we were not nearly as good as we wanted to be. The standard of player at the club did drop in that second season, and we went back almost to square one,' Smith observes. 'What that second year showed us early on was that things won't just happen for you – you have to get out there and make them happen. And it demonstrated to me that there was never any time for relaxation when you are part of a club such as Rangers. That's why we began the push for new players towards the turn of the year, and why we told the directors that more money had to be spent. We lost the league, in fact we were third [behind Celtic and Hearts], but we had a growing belief in the squad of players we were bringing together.'

Graham Roberts was destined for the exit door, in an episode highlighting the solidarity that existed between Souness and Smith. They were prepared to accept criticism of their strategies within the sanctity of the dressing room, but certainly not if a player threatened to spark anarchy at the workplace or, worse still, go public in the press about his dissatisfaction. The row erupted after a poor display from Rangers in going down to Aberdeen and after Smith, very matter-of-fact according to an individual who was there, questioned Roberts' culpability in conceding one of Aberdeen's goals. It started like any post-mortem, but the Englishman refused point-blank to accept that he might have been responsible, and as the language deterio-rated and tempers flared Souness walked in and asked what the f*** Roberts was complaining about, backing his assistant immediately. Reports claimed that Roberts and Souness traded punches – the truth, according to my source, is that they had to be pulled apart by other players or they would have brawled – but the result was that the men at the helm of Rangers glanced at each other, and in that instant and without any words needed, Roberts' fate was sealed. He did not help his cause by talking to the papers about the affair, then on the following Saturday at the final league game of the season against Falkirk, taking his seat in the stand among a large group of Rangers supporters, who cheered him to the rafters, and barracked Souness and Smith in the dugout. This was mutiny, and it was not as if Roberts was a 21-year-old ingenue, who might have been excused his intemperate behaviour on the grounds of immaturity. From Smith's perspective, if discipline broke down, everything else would collapse. His unflinching view of the business was:

> 'Managers cannot afford to walk away from difficult or unpopular judgments. Often things happen away from the public gaze which determine the direction you take, but if you bottle a tough disciplinary matter once, then you can lose *all* the players, and not just the one who brought the trouble to a head.'

Roberts was thrust on to the transfer market, and suffered professional humiliation for his trangressions. During the pre-season tour in the summer of 1988, Rangers' first-team squad travelled to Italy, but he was dispatched with the reserves on a low-key sojourn around the Highlands, instructions having been posted to the coaching staff that he was to strip as a substitute, but not be used in any of the matches. It was a stark reminder to him that no person was bigger than the club. It was also an indication that his bosses were growing more confident about the strength of the resources they had at their disposal. Ray Wilkins arrived from Paris for a cut-price £150,000, and developed into one of the best signings of that era, his positive attitude and never-say-die men-tality instantly endearing him to the Ibrox faithful. At New Year Mark Walters joined the ranks: he was another classy performer who would grow in stature throughout his time in Glasgow, not solely as a player, but as a man, given the racial abuse that he was forced to endure on travels across Scotland. Other useful perfor-mers pledged their allegiance to Souness: John Brown, a bullock-ing threat to those who dared impede his progress, a similar character in Ian Ferguson, England regular Gary Stevens, and Kevin Drinkell, who complemented an already potent attacking line-up. While none at Ibrox ever enjoyed a Celtic title celebration, there was a sense that the Bhoys had better savour their party, because the balance was shifting decisively away from Parkhead. As it transpired, seven years would elapse before Celtic again finished in the top two, let alone harboured serious pretensions of lifting the league championship. With the arrival of entrepreneur David Murray at the climax of 1988, the final pieces were efficiently fitted into a grand scheme which would delight Rangers followers, and depress those of Celtic.

CHAPTER SIX

MURRAY AND MO

❖

'I never thought that in my wildest dreams they would sign him'

Many words have been spouted about David Murray in the past two decades, laudatory and critical, reflecting contradictions in the businessman's personality. A committed individual who has transcended personal and family tragedy – his legs were amputated after a car crash, and he lost his wife to cancer – the Ayrshireman can be hugely protective of those he employs and respects; he can be surprisingly sentimental for someone whose concern is the balance sheet; and he can surprise even bitter opponents with his tireless innovation, industry and refusal to accept that any cause is lost. Alternatively, Murray can be a spiteful enemy, a man who bears grudges and spends an excessive amount of time checking out the backgrounds of those who dare to besmirch his name. He can also be pettily protectionist and ostrich-like, exemplified by his failure to tackle the scourge of sectarianism head-on when it was obvious that a section of the Ibrox support were bringing their club into disrepute as the 1990s progressed. But over the course of his stewardship as Rangers chairman – he bought the club from Lawrence Marlborough for £6m, and was unveiled in his new role on 23 October 1988 – precious few supporters have had genuine grounds for grievance. The now Sir David Murray may be found wanting if we scrutinise his words: 'Judge me on Europe', and there is little question that a man with such foresight in other areas should have created a youth academy sooner, but whatever his failings, Murray's arrival coincided with a golden era unfolding for Rangers.

From the start of the 1988–9 league campaign, prior to Murray's appointment, it had become clear that Celtic's achievement in winning the double in their centenary season had provided the dying gasps of a once-mighty organisation. From as early as the third game of the season, when Celtic travelled to Ibrox and were hammered 5-1, the gulf between the sides could not be disputed. This was Rangers' biggest winning margin in an Old Firm fixture for 28 years, testifying to the quality of the personnel who had now signed up. A couple of goals from Ally McCoist, a venomous volley from Ray Wilkins and strikes from Mark Walters and Kevin Drinkell highlighted their potency, and reduced Frank McAvennie's opening goal to a meaningless act of defiance. As soon as Terry Butcher looked over towards Celtic goalkeeper Ian Andrews before kick-off, and noted his glazed eyes, he fancied that a rout might be on. Similarly, former Scotland keeper Alan Rough, who had signed for Celtic during the summer, watched and marvelled at the spirit generated within the Rangers camp:

'Even the visitors had to grudgingly admit the power of the light-blue tidal wave which engulfed poor Andrews that day. Their ranks oozed with class and virtuosity, from Terry Butcher and Richard Gough in defence through to Wilkins, Ian Durrant and Ian Ferguson as the midfield enforcers, and McCoist, Walters and Drinkell up front, all of whom posed constant problems for Celtic. By comparison, Celtic weren't a great side. They were more workmanlike than inspired, and although they tried hard to stem the tide, they were never at the races. So it was an important afternoon, because there was just no arguing with the evidence that the balance was tilting decisively towards Rangers.'

By this stage the relationship between Graeme Souness and Walter Smith was operating like a well-oiled machine. Both knew their roles and where they had to be, knuckled down to their areas of expertise, and the symbiosis was sufficiently strong that they could go days without speaking, yet still know what the other was thinking. Their duties were subject to clear demarcation lines: so far as organisation at the grass-roots was concerned, Smith was the master of detail, accepting responsibility for much of the work which rarely earns recognition, but without which no club could hope to function smoothly. Within the training set-up, whether deploying various regimes so that players would not grow bored, Smith was in his element. He built a rapport with the playing staff and backroom employees which left the more aloof Souness free to concentrate on targeting signings, plotting tactical master-strokes and generally acting as Cock of the North. This suited them. Smith did not believe in the notion of joint managers, and his colleague had bigger ambitions than worrying about how the plastic cones should be arranged at practice sessions. While Smith was content to handle the chores, he was far more integral to Rangers' success than his self-effacing manner might have suggested. Both men were ultimately accountable for the success or otherwise of a team backed by substantial finance, and therefore every team selection and transfer signing involved a collaborative effort. Souness would enjoy the last say, but on most occasions he listened attentively to the contribution from his older partner.

All of which ensured that Rangers, who were developing the consistency which had eluded them in the previous two seasons, stretched away from their rivals in the championship race. They defeated Celtic in three of their four league encounters, including a first triumph at Parkhead in nine years, and after the arrival of David Murray set out on a rampant streak which brought them 14 wins in their last 16 matches, including nine consecutive victories. As if to emphasise the fashion in which the star-sprinkled team were primed to make grandiose statements, they lifted the domestic league trophy by a six-point margin over Aberdeen, totalling a record of 56 points and suffering just six defeats in 36 matches: this was in the days before three points were awarded for a win.

As Murray and Souness regularly made clear in their pronouncements, Europe was a massive priority, and when the team entered the UEFA Cup in the autumn of 1988, an auspicious challenge was anticipated. Rangers were pitted against GKS Katowice, and though a Mark Walters goal gave them only a slender lead before their journey to Poland, confidence within the squad remained high. The second leg was played at the Slaski Stadion in Chorzow, venue for an earlier European defeat to Gornik in 1969, and initially it seemed that Scottish optimism might be misplaced when Jan Furtok opened the scoring for GKS in the fourth minute with a curling free-kick. That merely served to galvanise Rangers, who mounted a sustained riposte and came close three times before Terry Butcher equalised with a fine header from a Walters corner in the 13th minute, and a Wilkins free-kick gained the lead four minutes later. Woods had to be in sublime form to thwart excellent efforts from Miroslaw Kubiztal and Krzysztof Walczak, and the hosts gained a temporary lifeline when the dangerous Kubiztal levelled matters shortly after the hour. But this was simply the precursor to Rangers finishing in barnstorming style, well-worked goals from Durrant and Ian Ferguson cementing a 5-2 aggregate success, and ensuring a relatively smooth passage into the second round, where they were drawn against familiar opponents in FC Koln. Rangers had met the German team three times before in their European history, and such a draw should have offered an alluring prospect, the chance to wipe the slate clean for their European Cup quarter-final defeat at the hands of these opponents in 1979. For the first time, however, Rangers were forced to realise that participating simultaneously in several tournaments carried drawbacks. Three days before their first-leg trip to the Stadion Mungersdorfer, Souness's troops joined battle with Aberdeen in the Scottish League Cup final, and though they clinched the trophy with a 3-2 win in a thrilling dénouement at Hampden Park, they paid for their exertions in the closing stages of a fraught tussle in Germany. Until the last 15 minutes the visitors were exemplary in terms of discipline and attacking intent, but the normally dependable McCoist squandered an opening. Legs grew weary as the clock ticked on, with the consequence that Olaf Janssen and Thomas Allofs found the net to leave Rangers facing an almighty struggle, a plight that was exacerbated when McCoist was ordered off in the dying seconds.

This match in some ways served as a template for many of Rangers' later European disappointments. The early promise, the signs of composure persuading fans to suppose that a goal would arrive if they remained patient . . . then the anti-climactic shattering of these hopes as the tide turned through self-inflicted error or a spark of world-class ability from an opponent. It was not as if FC Koln were anything more than a well-coached, modestly talented side with no great pretensions to featuring among the continental elite, but when they travelled to Glasgow with their significant lead, they found Rangers seriously weakened by the suspension of McCoist and Wilkins and injuries to Durrant and Brown. This should not have presented an insuperable obstacle to the team in clawing their way back into contention, but striking profligacy again cost them dear, and they were not helped when Walters crashed a 46th minute free-kick off the crossbar and Richard Gough hit the post with a 65th minute header. It was starting to develop into a wearily predictable pattern for Rangers, and though Drinkell broke the deadlock with a goal 15 minutes from the end, there was nothing else in the locker. Except, that is, from FC Koln, who sealed victory with a belated goal from the prolific Janssen. It was a deflating conclusion to an impressive display from Rangers for possibly 140 of the 180 minutes over two games, but there was nothing to be gained from seeking excuses about how the fixture list affected the club. After all, Dundee United had reached the UEFA Cup final in 1987 with a similar heavy schedule, and the Rangers' management duo had to accept responsibility for their refusal to countenance building two separate teams: one for domestic activity where the pace of every game was intense, the other designed for European action with skilful, multi-layered personnel in the mould of Brian Laudrup and Paul Gascoigne, who would eventually turn out for the club. Such a policy would have required a huge level of investment from Murray and his board, but the money was there at the end of the 1980s, and was never quite utilised to its full potential on the wider stage. All of which meant that Smith had to resort to using an uncharacter-istically porous argument in striving to defend Rangers' prob-lems in Europe:

> 'The players are being asked to do too much, it's as simple as that. At a club like Rangers the burdens are heavier, because we are enjoying a period of success which has seen us in League Cup finals and Scottish Cup finals as well as playing in Europe. We also have a fair number of international players, so you finish up with lads being asked to play 60 or 70 matches a season, and you soon discover that you cannot ask them to train too much during the week. It's impossible to do so. Asking players to do too much eventually damages them. It leads to more and more stress injuries, and it also damages them mentally.'

Some of this would have sounded a bit more convincing, but for the reality that Rangers seemed to want favours from clubs that they were stripping of their best players, at a stage in their history when most factors were in their favour. Celtic were on the wane, though they still managed to deny their traditional foes the treble by winning the Scottish Cup final 1-0, courtesy of a controversial goal when Roy Aitken took what should have been a Rangers throw-in and Joe Miller nipped in to score. Aberdeen, while still showing glimpses of their glory days under Alex Ferguson, were also not quite the force of old. As for Hearts and Hibs, more drama was being enacted off the pitch than on where the Edinburgh clubs were concerned. Rangers, in short, were sailing away into the distance in Scotland. Their policy was spend, spend, spend; they had a voluble manager, a multi-millionaire chairman, a swelling infrastructure and huge swathes of the west of Scotland where they could have charged almost anything in season ticket prices, just so long as Celtic were crushed. But Europe continued to be a baffling area, and one cannot escape the feeling that the club fell awkwardly between two stools when a more single-minded approach might have reaped dividends. The trouble was, and is, that European victories are not sufficient if Celtic, Hibs and Aberdeen are not being beaten on a regular basis. Souness did not square that circle.

❖

What Graeme Souness did succeed in doing was stirring up a hornets' nest in July of 1989 when, greeted by banner headlines normally reserved for presidential assassinations and royal deaths, Maurice Johnston, the controversial striker who had once head-butted the Ibrox team's Stuart Munro, confirmed that he was crossing the great divide by signing for Rangers. It was sensational stuff, for the self-styled Mojo was a Roman Catholic who had been pictured in May sporting a Celtic jersey as he stood beside manager Billy McNeill, and had proclaimed to reporters: 'It is a dream. I never thought they would want me back. I had offers from the Continent and England, but I wanted to wear the green and white again. Deep down, I have always wanted to be back at Celtic.' In cold print that seemed pretty conclusive, but the issue has become one of the most contentious incidents in the recent history of the Old Firm. At the heart of it was a bold step by Souness to erase at a stroke the traditional Rangers policy of not signing Catholic players. Why should the club be handicapped, he inquired early in his tenure, by being denied the opportunity to pick x or y simply because of their religion? Behind the scenes one or two Catholic players, such as John Spencer, were starting to emerge, but Souness recognised that he could inflict a double whammy by shattering the old taboo and embarrassing those in charge at Celtic Park, if he

79

could entice Johnston to the club. The player had written in his autobiography: 'Let me just spell out where I stand here. I am a Celtic man through and through, and so dislike Rangers because they are a force in Scottish football and a threat to the club I love. But more than that, I hate the religious policy which they still maintain. Why won't they sign a Roman Catholic? I hate religious bigotry, and the Rangers fans always tried to single me out [for special abuse] in Old Firm games.' As usual with the two Glasgow clubs, outlandish notions exist as to how the deal came about. But the most likely chain of events is that Souness had made contact with his target before Johnston was paraded by Celtic, which suggests that that occasion was little more than a disastrous PR stunt, which backfired. Terry Butcher, who had locked horns with Johnston during the Scotland v England match won 1-0 by his team, suggests that Mo wasn't exactly shy about his plans:

'At one point, I asked: "So you're coming back to Scotland next season?"

'"Yeah," he replied. "I will be with you next season."

'I responded: "Yes, and I am looking forward to giving you a good kicking."

'"But he looked at me a little quizzically, and answered: "No, I will be playing with you."

'Had I been really sharp, I would have picked it up, yet I dismissed it as the usual ramblings of a centre-forward trying to put me off my game. But it was true.'

It is understandable why Celtic responded so badly, and with such sustained lack of grace, to the manner in which one of their former heroes had slipped through their grasp. But that still does not undermine the stance adopted by Souness, who had previously striven to bring Ray Houghton to Ibrox without success, and who was painfully aware that Johnston's signing would create ructions. Hence the plethora of meetings involving Souness, Smith and Murray as they discussed all the possible ramifications of the deal coming to fruition. As Smith explained, all three were in favour of proceeding with the move, but they were not so naïve as to pretend that it would not cause shock waves within Scottish football and beyond. They had to wonder how the player himself might react to sectarian outbursts from the worst elements in both enclaves. As they weighed up the considerations, none of them was concerned about how Celtic might react, and why should they have been? In plain terms, the player had been to Celtic Park for talks, had maintained that he would sign, and he had posed for the media wearing a Celtic jersey. Ultimately he had not signed any forms and he was not a Celtic player, though if chairman Jack McGinn had conducted the formalities appropriately, he might well have secured his man. As it stands, there is sufficient evidence to support the notion that Souness had sounded out Johnston prior to the media occasion at Celtic Park, and that when McGinn & Co procrastinated, it was the last straw. Celtic had been gazumped.

The most predictable response to this taboo-shattering story hitting the headlines was the sound of fury, which ultimately did not signify that much, but was indicative of the deep passions which lurked in normally sober people when the natural order of their world was turned upside down. David Miller, general secretary of the Rangers Supporters' Association, offered this opinion: 'I never thought in my wildest dreams that they would sign him. Why sign him above all others? There will be a lot of people handing back their season tickets. I don't want to see a Roman Catholic at Ibrox. Rangers have always stood for one thing, and the biggest majority of fans have been brought up with a true-blue team.'

Meanwhile, as a staff writer on the recently launched newspaper *Scotland on Sunday*, I visited my birthplace of Whitburn, West Lothian, and sought a variety of views on the Johnston business, with alarmingly depressing consequences. Bobbie R [who refused to give his surname] said that 'hell would freeze over' before he would ever return to Ibrox and 'put money into that wee Fenian bastard's back pocket'. Peter Brown, a 29-year-old joiner who described himself as being 'not interested in religion', changed tack somewhat when MoJo was mentioned: 'That wee c*** is a money grabbing piece of s***, and he should f*** off back to the Tims, because we dinnae want him at Rangers.' My third interviewee, 64-year-old Margaret Crawford, hummed and hawed prior to confiding that she couldn't care less about football. But her views on the bold Maurice were, in certain respects, even creepier: "He's just no' one of us, know what I mean? He's a Pape, he thinks differently from us, and we are Protestants for a reason, you know. That mob didnae even support us in the Second World War; they went bleating off to the enemy, and I've never forgiven the Fenians for that.' Later, in the Cross Tavern, I heard that a man had strolled up to another at the bar, punched him in the face and shouted: 'That's for f***ing Mo Johnston. Then he walked out, and the barman explained: 'Och, that's just Archie.'

Vitriol manifested itself throughout the west of Scotland and beyond, but gradually it became clear that Souness, Smith and Murray had calculated correctly that they could live without a few bigots who might tear up their season tickets – just one book was returned – and that plenty of opportunities would arise for Johnston to silence his critics where it genuinely mattered. In essence, a few burned scarves and a collection of expletive-laden letters to Ibrox should not be allowed to halt the march of progress any more than the death threats to Johnston which were made to newspaper offices – mostly from pubs, one suspects. Granted, there was the absurd spectacle of Rangers' kit man Jimmy Bell refusing to acknowledge his existence, while at mealtimes a number of the Scottish players preferred not to sit with Johnston. When the club attempted to hold a press conference on their pre-season tour of Italy, to endorse his arrival, there was no problem with such as Wilkins, Woods and Walters, whereas most of the Scots in the squad declined to attend. But Souness was utterly unflinching in his resolve. It was his finest hour at Ibrox.

❖

Amid the fuss, Rangers had to concentrate on launching a league title defence, and they began in stuttering fashion by losing to St Mirren and Hibs in their opening fixtures as the prelude to pitching up at Parkhead, where those affable characters inhabiting the old Jungle section of the ground screamed out relentless abuse at Johnston for a full hour-and-a-half. This was complemented by some hissing and booing from a section of the Rangers support, which did not relent even after Butcher sent the visitors ahead. But credit where credit is due: there was no shortage of courage in Johnston's handling of the experience, explaining why more discerning observers swiftly reached the conclusion that they might never be able to fall in love with MoJo, but they could respect his ability, appreciate that he had shown guts by crossing the line, and cheer politely. As frequently happens in sporting endeavours, within a couple of months of being pilloried, Johnston survived and prospered. His goal helped Rangers to defeat close challengers Aberdeen, his scoring sequence continued against Hearts, Dundee United, St Mirren and Hibs, and even the most taciturn traditionalists could be heard to mutter in their beer variations on the theme of: 'Aye, he's a Pape, but he's our f***ing Pape, and the Celts are no' getting their hands on him.' Irrational of course, but so much of sport cannot be defined in logical terms, and it seemed almost inevitable that Johnston would score against his former team when Celtic arrived at Ibrox for the second Old Firm derby of the 1989–90 campaign, the first having finished 1-1. He did just that! His intervention came with the deadlock unbroken, and as both sets of fans were starting to settle for another share of the spoils. Johnston latched on to a loose clearance at the edge of the Copland Road penalty-area, and dispatched a powerful right-foot shot into the corner of the net. In an instant he rushed towards the crowd, and he was mobbed by a congregation of euphoric Rangers hailing him as their hero. The goal helped to accelerate Rangers towards another title, and made a massive dent in whatever optimism remained in Celtic hearts. Rangers continued to strengthen the team with the likes of Trevor

Steven and Nigel Spackman, who clinched victory at Celtic Park in their first New Year victory at the ground since 1964. The Ibrox club could even afford a mini-slump in March, when they went five matches without a victory, without letting it disturb their equilibrium. It was typical of the contrasting fortunes being experienced by the Glasgow clubs that Rangers restored their poise with a 3-0 win of such a comprehensive nature against Celtic that the date, April Fools' Day, seemed fitting for the vanquished. A Butcher cross struck Anton Rogan's hand and Walters hit the penalty home; Johnston added a second, and McCoist completed the demolition. Wrapping up the title was a formality, and the job was concluded briskly at Tannadice on 21 April with a Trevor Steven goal as the catalyst for the partying to commence. Sadly, it was not sufficient that Rangers had been thoroughly professional in their campaign, the hour of triumph was clouded by contoversy. With their guard down, the champions were foolish enough to partake of a few alcoholic beverages while still ensconced in the Dundee United changing rooms, and subsequently decided to let rip with a collection of Rangers songs, including *The Sash*, a popular anthem among Orangemen. Predictably, a BBC television crew were on hand to relay pictures to an unimpressed nation, which must have been infuriating to Souness, in particular, considering his attempts to exorcise such demons from his side.

Other problems proved just as obdurate, most notably the club's failure to make an impression on European ventures. They were drawn against the formidable Bayern Munich in September 1989, and though the first leg was at Ibrox, that did not faze the German maestros. With an accomplished and clinical showing, they effectively killed off the tie in Glasgow, recovering from losing an early goal, a Walters penalty, before Ludwig Kogl equalised after half-an-hour and the Bavarians produced a resplendent second-half display with goals from Olaf Thon and Klaus Agenthaler, which left Rangers 3-1 down. It was a disappointing performance, admittedly against opponents of fine quality, but doubly frustrating was Rangers securing a goalless draw in the return leg, which would have been a creditable achievement had they not relinquished the initiative so emphatically in front of their own fans. In the build-up to these major European occasions, tension gripped the Souness demeanour, which suggested that he realised the club could stack up as many domestic prizes as they wished, but would be judged only on the wider stage. Walter Smith sympathised with this predicament, yet as one who was close to the Rangers fans, he appreciated that no excuses or alibis would be accepted by followers with the attitude: we have triumphed in Europe in the past without the resources we have now, so we should be capable of succeeding these days. No matter that the management could justifiably claim that many of the best European sides had transformed themselves totally between 1972 and '90, the supporters were entitled to their opinion.

Quite apart from Souness acquiring the knack of being able to turn a kerfuffle into a full-scale row, having fallen out with among others Ally McCoist (whom he stuck on the bench and tried to offload to Sunderland), Scottish Television, Terry Butcher (who moved on to Coventry) the SFA and even the tea lady at St Johnstone, the manager must have recognised that he was no longer the exciting new kid on the block by the time his side were drawn against the powerful Red Star Belgrade in the second round of the 1990-91 European Cup. It was a treacherous proposition given the pedigree of the opposition, and though Mark Hateley had joined Rangers from Monaco in a £1m transfer, the scale of the task was illustrated when Smith, who had travelled to watch Red Star in action, returned to Glasgow and uttered just one word, of the four-letter variety, to Souness. Unsurprisingly, considerable apprehension was noted among players and fans as they embarked on the flight to the Balkans, and one follower on the journey, Rangers' historian Robert McElroy, was suitably impressed by the hosts:

'Smith's feelings of foreboding were well founded. In the first leg, Red Star tore the visitors apart with their class and pace, watched by 82,500 packing the sprawling bowl that is their very own "Maracana" stadium. Souness's team selection puzzled many onlookers, two wingers having been included, namely Mark Walters and Pieter Huistra, in the absence of Hateley. The nightmare began in just the eighth minute, when the pace of Dusko Radinovic tore the left flank of Rangers' defence asunder, his low cross being diverted into his own net by John Brown.

'The Light Blues were being overrun by the Slavs, with the class and speed of Robert Prosinecki, Dragisa Binic and Darko Pancev showing them to be a class apart. Somehow, by dint of good fortune and outstanding goalkeeping on the part of Chris Woods, Rangers survived without further loss as the clock ticked past the hour mark. Indeed, Rangers seemed to be gaining a foothold in the game when a superb free-kick by Prosinecki found the net, via an upright, after 65 minutes, with serious questions being asked about the discipline of the wall and the positioning of the goalkeeper. Seven minutes later, Huistra should have secured a priceless away goal, heading wide when it seemed easier to score, and in their very next attack Red Star surged up the park for Pancev to take clinical advantage of hesitation on the part of Gough.'

This was a 3-0 defeat which could have been 6-0 or 7-1, and there was nothing to do but applaud the mastery of the victors. Souness, who was normally an upbeat and robust individual, looked close to being crushed, lamenting to journalists at Belgrade Airport: 'How can I possibly win the European Cup with 11 Scots in the team?' It was a feeble comment to offer, considering that the side he had sent out to tackle Red Star contained six non-Scots in the guise of five English players and Huistra, and that Souness had been at Ibrox for more than four years and, given his foreign contacts, could surely have bolstered his squad with French, Italian or German players. But the weariness of his remark was an indication that no individual can rage against the world forever without hitting a wall. Souness and his team managed minor redemption in the second leg when they restricted Red Star to a 1-1 draw, the goals springing from Pancev and McCoist, but there was no disguising the truth that this was a watershed. It was the beginning of the end for Souness.

CHAPTER SEVEN

A DREAM COME TRUE

❖

'He couldn't have made a better choice'

As Graeme Souness discovered during his spell in Scottish football, garnering respect, even grudging, can be a difficult task. The Ibrox throng could admire him for resuscitating their beloved club, but that did not mean they were prepared to take him to their hearts or to like him particularly, whereas Walter Smith was swiftly acknowledged as the true heartbeat of the Rangers empire. Ewan Prentice, a long-time Rangers supporter, wrote to me when he learned that I was writing this book, and his words on the disparate nature of the two management figures reflect sound common sense. He homes in on Smith in the first instance:

'He was one of us. We watched him at matches, and he went through the hundred little agonies which we did in the stands when a player misses a sitter or makes a bad challenge or gets smacked, off the ball, by an opponent, and that was one of the biggest differences between Walter and Souness. With the latter, there was always the sense of a volcano about to blow its stack, but not to anything specific – he was just an angry bugger with a bad temper and a huge ego who thought every referee and linesman was against him. We didn't mind when Souness first began bringing the big names to Glasgow. We would have been daft to have rejected the opportunity to have big Terry [Butcher]

Left. Starting out: the young Walter Smith soon recognised he was not a world-class footballer, but lacked for nothing in work ethic and determination (*D.C. Thomson*).

Below. Resisting the 'Tic: Smith offered yeoman service for Dundee United in his playing days and here, in the 1974 Scottish Cup final, stems the threat of two Celtic legends David Hay and Kenny Dalglish (*SNS Group*).

Above. The Tannadice Two: Walter Smith and the Dundee United manager, Jim McLean, plot further European success for their flourishing club (*D.C. Thomson*).

Below. A Pair of Greats: Walter Smith joined forces with Alex Ferguson to lead Scotland to the 1986 World Cup finals in Mexico, following the death of Jock Stein. The duo later worked together at Old Trafford (*SNS Group*).

above. Fire and frost: Graeme Souness and Walter Smith were hugely contrasting personalities, but their partnership sparked a glorious resurgence at Rangers when they joined forces in 1986 (*Newsquest Media Group*).

below. In the Ibrox tradition: Three of the stalwarts in the history of Rangers FC come together as Walter Smith banters with the club's former manager Jock Wallace and a youthful Ally McCoist joins in the repartee (*Newsquest Media Group*).

ft. No Mo' Blues: He was the most controversial signing in Rangers' history, but Mo Johnston, e former Celtic pin-up boy who crossed the great divide, soon became a hit with the fervent rox support (*Scotsman Publications*).

ove. Pieces of Silver: Walter Smith and Archie Knox, two men with granite in their veins, on began collecting silverware when they teamed up at Ibrox, winning the domestic treble in 93 (*Scotsman Publications*).

low. Smart men: Andy Goram, 'The Goalie', another Rangers hero, who was pivotal to the b's Nine-In-A-Row triumph. Here the men show off the Player of the Year and Manager of the ar awards for the 1992–3 season (*Scotsman Publications*).

Above. Gazza job: Paul Gascoigne was rarely out of the headlines during his time in Glasgow, but although not all the publicity was favourable, few people could deny that he had magic in his boots (*Newsquest Media Group*).

Below. Cheers!: Walter Smith and Archie Knox have often been perceived as being dour characters. But in the heat of the battle, both men relished the thrill of the chase, as witnessed in this dug-out delight (*Newsquest Media Group*).

Opposite. Hammer of the Hoops: A grateful manager embraces Jorg Albertz, an iconic player who often reserved his best for Old Firm derbies. This time he celebrates scoring against Celtic the 1998 Scottish Cup semi-final. (*Scotsman Publications*).

Above. Prize possessions: There were some who claimed that Walter Smith was lucky to enjoy so much success in his first spell at Rangers but his troubled spell at Everton had some high points as the Manager of the Month award attests (*Trinity Mirror plc*).

Below. Tough at the top: Life wasn't always rosy for Smith and Knox as they pursued their careers south of the border. Here, a pensive Smith and Archie Knox show the strains connected with the Liverpool derby (*Trinity Mirror plc*).

bove. Your country needs you!: Walter Smith inherited a mess from Berti Vogts when he ecame the Scotland manager in 2004. But soon enough, he started to turn things round and ake Scottish supporters feel proud of their team again. (*SNS Group*).

elow. A new mood: The Scots, under Vogts, had slipped to embarrassing depths in the FIFA nkings. But Smith re-ignited the country's passion and here shares a joke with one of his edecessors, Craig Brown, as Scotland dared to dream again (*SNS Group*).

Above. In Old Firm hands: As Scotland started recording some impressive results, most notably 1-0 victory over the mighty France at Hampden, the good work done by Smith and his Old Firm confreres, Ally McCoist and Tommy Burns, became obvious (*Newsquest Media Group*).

Below. You CAN go back: Walter Smith was accused by some Scotland fans of betrayal when he quit Scotland to rejoin troubled Rangers. But Smith had always insisted that he desired a return to club management, so the allegations didn't stick (*Newsquest Media Group*).

Opposite. Here's to the future: Since Walter Smith returned to Rangers, he and captain, Barry Ferguson, have been instrumental in effecting a resurgence, including victories over the French and German title winners in the 2007 Champions League (*SNS Group*).

Above. My own private heaven: Walter Smith could hardly have believed, when he left Rangers in 1998, that he would one day return to Ibrox. Here he is, back at the club he supported as a boy and ready for the fresh challenges that lie ahead (*Newsquest Media Group*).

and Chrissy [Woods] at Ibrox, but I don't know how much success he would have had without Smith working away behind the scenes.

'Certainly, you never got the impression when you listened to Souness that he was wasting too much time studying videos or chalking up tactical formations on blackboards. It was as if he was more interested in the strut and leading with the chin, than actually getting his hands dirty. We tolerated that, of course, because Rangers won trophies again under his command, but me and my mates weren't fooled by all the bullshit. Losing [Graham] Roberts needn't have happened, but we thought: "Oh well, we have plenty of other options." Then when Terry fell out with Souness as well, we started to think to ourselves: "Hang on, everybody else can't always be wrong in these disputes." And that scepticism built up, month by month, especially when we heard that Souness didn't fancy McCoist and wanted to get rid of him as well. I mean, McCoist! Super Ally! He was a bloody talisman for us, and anybody who didn't appreciate that fact simply had no real understanding of Rangers FC.'

The antipathy between Souness and McCoist could not have been more glaring, at least on the management side. Quite simply, every time he marched into the dressing room and noted the easy charm which McCoist possessed in abundance, it was like a red rag, the more so because when he had initially arrived at Ibrox, Souness was determined that every major signing, every high-profile recruit, everybody who was anybody within the club, would dance to the same tune. Dissent was not tolerated. Anyone who stood up to him was sent packing, if not to another club, then to the bench or the reserves, where any talented footballer hates languishing. In the early days the manager had the power and the authority to make these rules stick, but the longer he remained in office the more obvious it became to players and fans that Souness had drive and desire, but could not be described as lovable. Not even remotely. McCoist, on the other hand, was the sort of personality who had a twinkle in his eye and could even induce a smile in a Celtic supporter, and that infuriated Souness almost as much as the fact that *'Super Ally!'* soon turned into a familiar chant at matches. Richard Gough often saw player and manager at close quarters in situations where Walter Smith would be forced into the role of conciliator and peacemaker. After a 2-0 defeat at Celtic Park on 2 January 1988, the full extent of Souness's dismissive attitude towards his striker erupted: he regarded him as not fit to lace Kenny Dalglish's boots, and McCoist does not dispute the point. Gough provides the details:

'That was my first game at Celtic, and they were playing well at the time and we were struggling a bit. Our side was changing week in, week out and Graeme picked himself and said: "I'll take care of Paul McStay, no problem." I loved it when he said that, but McStay was magnificent in that match; he ran the show and we were beaten comfortably. Anyway, as soon as the game finished, Graeme tore into the dressing room and went through every one of us like a dose of salts. He said to Chris Woods: "You're the f***ing England goalkeeper? You're a *girl*." Then he slaughtered Gary Stevens, and killed me. No one was spared. He said we were all a bunch of women, we had no heart, or nothing. Then he got to McCoist, who was hurting badly enough in any case, because he had had one of his quieter games. Souness turned to him and bawled out: "You were a dud at St Johnstone, you were a dud with Sunderland reserves, and you're a dud here. There were 22 players out there, and you were the f***ing worst of the lot of them."

'Coisty was shivering with emotion, nearly crying, and eventually he shot up to his feet and shouted: "I wasn't the worst. *You* were!" Then all hell broke loose, and Graeme had Ally round the throat until we all dived in and separated them. Then we climbed on to a very quiet team bus. It was like a morgue on that journey.'

Eighteen months into his tenure, Souness could behave in this fashion without incurring any penalty. But as Smith sought out

McCoist to reassure him that he had at least one fan in the managerial ranks, similar instances of needless machismo and negative publicity kept filtering out to the paying customers, whose early praise for Souness altered into carping about his endlessly confrontational style. This meant little to the man at the centre of the issue, but Smith heard the whispers of discontent on the periphery, and eventually negotiated a path off the bench for McCoist, whose goals started to stack up again. Their relationship, which blossomed as the years passed, is based on three factors: a shared love affair for Rangers and everything connected with the club; an appreciation that football serves up a variety of experiences ensuring good and bad days, the trick being not to let travails supersede the triumphs; and that there is no shame in not succeeding if you have gone into an adventure with 100 per cent courage, commitment and camaraderie. It's a straightforward philosophy, perhaps based on the men's working-class roots, but it also revolves around feeling blessed to be able to enjoy a career in football and that, whatever might transpire, this is no environment for po-faced mercenaries. Hence the deliberate delivery that Smith employs for banter, an instance of which came on a morning that McCoist turned up late for a training session (again): 'This is simply not good enough, Ally. You'll miss your own funeral at this rate. If everybody else can be here on the dot, why can't you?' McCoist made a show of consulting his watch, interrupted Smith in mid-flow, and responded loftily: 'I think you'll find, boss, that this is the *earliest* I've ever been late.' No answer to that.

By 1991 it was apparent that Souness had achieved as much as he could at Rangers. The club had whimpered out of Europe at the hands of Red Star Belgrade, and despite a regular influx of expensive new signings, including the acquisition of Mark Hateley from AC Milan for £1m, their league form was more juggernaut than Rolls-Royce, closer to a prosaic score-one-and-win mantra than the free-flowing football which supporters craved. Souness was orchestrating his exit strategy, en route to the familiar surroundings of Anfield. On a fog-laden February Tuesday in Glasgow, he and Smith met in the Bellahouston Hotel for a sauna, a couple of soft drinks and a chat about life in general. Conversation switched abruptly into serious mode when Souness announced that he had been offered the Liverpool management job, following the resignation of Kenny Dalglish. Smith was taken aback, not so much by the revelation as by the fact that his colleague, who was normally so confident in his abilities, sounded slightly apprehensive about whether he should accept the job. The obvious questions came: 'Walter, what do you think? Should I stay or should I go?' Smith, who could have regarded this issue as an irrelevance or as an opportunity to encourage Souness to quit Rangers in the expectation that he would take over the top job, went home, thought carefully about the situation, and arranged to catch up with Souness the next day. He then responded with a cogent, well-researched argument that Souness should decline the Anfield post. His reasons were persuasive: Liverpool had slipped into decline from the mighty force they had been in the early- and mid-1980s, some of their more exalted players were close to being over the hill, and not a lot of money was available to replace them. Nor would the supporters tolerate any kind of expanded rebuilding programme over five or even three years.

Once Souness had listened patiently, he appeared to have grasped the message that this job had all the potential of a poisoned chalice. Within a few days he let Smith know that he had turned down Liverpool, and that it was business as usual at Rangers. Whether either really believed this is open to question, and one of the 1991 team told me that most of the Rangers squad were praying that Souness would go:

'The Red Star defeat was pretty devastating. It wasn't as if we should have gone into that match afraid of the opposition, but we were all over the place tactically, and they showed that we were a long way behind the best European teams in terms of pace or vision, or even being able to move the ball quickly out of defence.

Afterwards Souness had the look of a man who knew basically that he was f***ed. He had been given a fantastic chance by Rangers, but he had also been told by David Murray that it wasn't enough for the Gers to be strong in Scotland; they had to be a major force on the Continent as well, and I don't think he had a clue as to how to make that happen. The thing was that if we had become a fabulously entertaining team on the domestic circuit and we had been knocking five, six, seven goals past Hearts, Hibs and Celtic every week, the supporters might just have been satisfied to be kings of their own jungle, because I knew from talking to guys at the supporters' clubs that they weren't obsessed with climbing to the top in Europe. If you gave these lads a choice of four wins a season against Celtic or a European Cup final appearance, I know which the majority of them would have chosen. So they had their priorities, and whether they were right or wrong, at least they stuck to them. Souness, on the other hand, seemed to be all over the place by 1991.'

The man was certainly not intent on loitering long in Glasgow. Although his initial rejection of Liverpool's approach was made public to notably mixed reviews, newspapers north and south of the Border continued to speculate that he was simply negotiating an enhanced deal, and Merseyside radio stations reported on his movements as if he had signed the new contract. Three weeks after his initial conversation with Smith and with Rangers now having become embroiled in a fraught battle for the Scottish League title with Aberdeen, the two were flying to London to check out a couple of prospective signings when Souness confirmed that Liverpool had made a second bid for his services. With no trace of the indecisiveness which had marked his previous reaction, he told Smith that he had taken the job, and he would leave Rangers as soon as convenient. This provoked conflicting emotions in his companion, but further information provided a jolt for Smith. As they flew over Heathrow Airport, Souness announced: 'I have big plans for Liverpool, Walter. And I want you to come down with me to

Anfield, and be my assistant.' Smith was tempted . . . for roughly half-a-second. The money would have been good, as always with Souness, but significant considerations outweighed a bounteous bank balance. Everything that Smith held dear, namely his family, friends and football club, were in Glasgow. He belonged there, the city was in his blood, and the reservations that he had expressed about Liverpool to Souness still applied. Smith could envisage problems for a football figure heading to Anfield as an assistant, and being asked to transform the hierarchy of the fabled Boot Room. If he was being honest with himself, Walter Smith was also fed up being second-in-command. That might have suited him at Dundee United and in his introduction to employment at Ibrox, but he was now 43 and had built up more than 15 years in a variety of coaching positions. He did not have to make excuses to anyone, hence his reflection on his decisive response to decline the Souness invitation:

'No matter how much I had enjoyed the roller-coaster years of working with him, I just didn't want to leave Rangers. My heart was at Ibrox. It had been since the first time I ever walked through the gates as a wee boy, and that was incredibly important to me. Graeme understood my point of view, and although he was disappointed, we both knew what we had to do.'

Despite weeks of intrigue, Souness had neglected to inform David Murray of his imminent intention to decamp to Anfield, but then the Glasgow rumour mill is never stilled or silent. One Friday evening prior to a match Smith received a phone call from the chairman, who asked directly: "Do you know about Graeme going to Liverpool?" The question could have placed Smith in an invidious position. If he answered honestly, Murray might suspect him of plotting behind his back, and if he was less than truthful, that could rebound on him. As was his wont, Smith plumped for candour, and replied: 'Yes, he has talked to me about it.' Murray, who had suspected as much, then displayed no-nonsense leadership qualities, while Souness attempted to cling on at Ibrox until the end of the season, to collect another trophy. That scenario might well have suited the outgoing manager, but it definitely did not sit well with Murray. He was a close friend who was entitled to feel if not betrayed, then disgruntled at the covert manner in which discussions had been progressing for the best part of a month. There could be no more dithering, no more media speculation, hence his decision to inform Souness that he should clear his desk and vacate his post with immediate effect. No matter that the story hit the headlines at an inopportune moment for Rangers – the club were stricken with a lengthening injury list, and coming under increasing pressure from Aberdeen – Murray's reasoning was that once a man had committed himself to another club, particularly one such as Liverpool that required instant remedial treatment, it did no one any favours to have him lingering for a week, even a few days. In April 1991, just as had occurred when Souness arrived at Ibrox and also when Mo Johnston was unveiled in a Rangers jersey, the club were suddenly propelled into a whirlwind of hype and hysteria. It was to their advantage that during the more extravagant flights of fancy, one man remained stubbornly down to earth, and Murray realised that Smith ticked all the right boxes. He was talented, astute, receptive to new ideas but a traditionalist at heart, a warm and engaging presence for the youngsters in the squad, who termed him Uncle Walter. A big brother for the older lads, he could engage with them in droll patter or full-strength industrial invective, whatever was required, and his loyalty to Rangers was paramount.

Other names were mentioned, and for a few days after Souness's peremptory exit Kenny Dalglish was front-runner at 4-1, with Smith down the list at 7-1 behind Alex Ferguson at 5-1, who had yet to make magic at Manchester United. What most of the punters did not realise was that Murray had spent all of 24 hours mulling over a replacement before engaging with Smith after a match at Ibrox, and presenting the simple message: 'If you want the job, you can have it.' It may not seem the most enthusiastic offer, but what both personalities knew was that some questions can be answered only in the affirmative, and this was assuredly one of them. Smith certainly did not have to concern himself with people quibbling over his selection, and he was acclaimed as the natural choice by most observers. The response of the man himself:

'Anybody who has stood in the crowd at Ibrox as a six-year-old, and felt like I was in heaven, will know what was going through my mind. It felt like a dream come true. But of course there were other things to worry about as well.'

John Greig's reaction:

'When David Murray told me he was appointing Walter to take over from Graeme, I told him he couldn't have made a better choice. Walter had worked closely with the players during his time in charge, and he had earned their respect – but he was smart enough to recognise that all good teams need to keep evolving.'

Craig Brown, at that stage the Scotland assistant manager, recalls similarly effusive feelings:

'Sometimes, after a period when there is a lot of unrest and you have gone through a revolution, you need somebody to bring stability to the table, and Walter was one of the calmest people in a crisis you could ever imagine. I recall meeting him a few weeks after he had been appointed Rangers boss, and he was bristling with purpose, and he looked as if he couldn't wait to get down to business with his team, his methods. That was no slur on Graeme, but rather that when you are the No. 2, there are always those who wonder if you can make it as a No. 1. He soon showed them.'

Walter Smith thrived in testing circumstances when a combination of managerial turmoil and a weakened squad might easily have allowed Aberdeen to break the Old Firm's recent stranglehold on the title. Smith's first match in charge was against St Mirren in Paisley, and despite an error-strewn performance from the visitors, Sandy Robertson's goal was sufficient to seal victory. Dundee United were defeated at Ibrox, but as that success was being celebrated, Richard Gough went down with hepatitis, and the scale of injury and illness was such that Smith confessed: 'For a couple of days we were genuinely struggling to put a team together.' Critics would maintain that the club were to blame as they should have had ample resources at their disposal, but all Smith could do was drag out the sticking plaster, ask the physios about best- and worst-case prognoses, and cast his eye over the reserves in case a teenager or two could be pressed into service in the final two matches of the championship. Aberdeen must still be kicking themselves at their profligacy, when it might have been simpler for them to wrap up a title triumph which few could honestly have begrudged them. In the lead up to the showdown between the main rivals, Smith's men were trounced 3-0 by Motherwell at Fir Park, while the Dons stretched their 12-match unbeaten sequence with a win over St Johnstone, which installed them at the top of the table, and guaranteed that a draw would suffice when they came calling at Ibrox the following weekend. This was the closest finish to a campaign since the dramatic events of 1986, when Hearts delivered the trophy into Celtic's grasp, and as Smith plotted in the short term, he recruited an assistant from Manchester United, the familiar figure of Archie Knox, the coup creating a temporary chill in relations with Alex Ferguson, who was less than impressed at losing his invaluable colleague while preparing for the European Cup-Winners' Cup final against Barcelona in Rotterdam. Smith was as surprised as anyone that Knox took the bait, after he had sounded out Ray Wilkins without success, but these two characters were hewn from granite, would never waste their breath on flowery language when straightforward signals would do the trick, and they worked instinctively from the outset. The empathy, which had to be witnessed to be believed, meant that each could end the other's sentences, and that Smith could walk away from a conversation and return a few minutes later, and pick up on the thread that Knox had sewn. A terrific party trick if the football work dried up!

What was immediately evident to these wily operators was the need to make changes during the summer break, but the priority was striving to clinch Rangers' third consecutive league title. It might have been a tall order in other circumstances, but Aberdeen were no longer as confident on their travels to Glasgow as they had been under the maestro Fergie, and though they carved out a substantial number of chances, lack of composure and a killer instinct cost them dear. Mark Hateley, who had been written off prematurely by some when he toiled to adapt to the pace of the Scottish game during early outings, had established himself as a potent attacking threat in the air or at close quarters, and Aberdeen were left cursing the Englishman's name, and mourning their loss of a wonderful chance of the championship, as he twice pounced to secure a 2-0 victory for Rangers. It was an afternoon of conflicting emotions for Smith. He accepted the applause, but ultimately understood that this was not his team: 'I didn't look on it as my first trophy as a manager, because I didn't feel I could do that when it was clear that I had only been in charge for the last few matches of the season. Mind you, I knew deep down that if we had lost against Aberdeen that day, then it would have been looked on as the first trophy I had lost as a manager.'

Relief pervaded Ibrox as much as any emotion. By now Celtic were in such a poor state that their supporters' humour tended to be of the gallows variety. As for Aberdeen, who had provided such a stubborn and sustained challenge on a budget a tenth or so of that available to Rangers, they would not provide such a potent threat again for many years. Over in Edinburgh Hearts and Hibs were at each other's throats over Wallace Mercer's controversial proposal to create one capital side, which would have had the unfortunate effect of consigning the Easter Road club to oblivion. Given these circumstances, Rangers had the scope for expansion that had never quite materialised under Souness, and Smith was already planning for future challenges, even if there was one final communiqué to his former Ibrox associate, which he could relish:

> 'The dust had barely settled on the Aberdeen victory, when Graeme phoned me in the manager's office after the game to congratulate me and the players on the victory. When I told him the team that had finished the match that afternoon, he wouldn't believe me, because we had so many people operating out of position, and yet we still held on for the title. It gave me the basis for the changes which I knew I had to make the following season, but it also proved to me that there was a vibrancy and a resilience about this particular Rangers squad, which would see them through thick and thin.'

Many taxing episodes were in store for Smith and Knox, not least in tackling the conundrum of how to prosper in Europe and to continue to dominate domestic matters. Smith clocked up hundreds of miles on scouting assignments, speaking to a raft of agents about players who might bring something special to the Rangers cause. He also demonstrated that while he was nowhere near as in-your-face as Souness, his hunger for football prizes was acute, and his words emphasise also that he has not strayed far from his origins:

> 'It has just always been there, the desire to win, and the bringing together of a collection of individuals into a successful team, and that was my main task at Rangers. My desire to be the best doesn't just stop at football. If I am involved in anything competitive, I like to win, and it's actually winning that keeps me going and allows me to keep working. Not too many other people are in that position, and I count my blessings. A lot of my pals in football

haven't been quite as fortunate as me, and I learned a long time ago exactly how hard they had to work to achieve anything in the game. As football managers, we are lucky because of the rewards and benefits we receive that are denied people in this country – who are unemployed, for instance.'

CHAPTER EIGHT

A CANNY PATH FROM
TRADITION TO TRANSITION

❖

'He fostered a shared purpose among all the guys'

When he succeeded Graeme Souness in the major role at Rangers FC, Walter Smith could not have been accused of letting the grass grow under his feet. He had scrutinised the squad and assessed resources barely before celebrations had finished to mark a third league title in a row, and he reached the conclusion that he would need to inject some fresh blood and increase the number of Scots-born personnel, given a new UEFA clampdown on teams deploying foreign mercenaries rather than promoting home-grown talent. Since Souness's policy of enticing a string of English players had become counter-productive – Mark Hateley had been forced to watch from the stand on a number of instances during the previous European Cup campaign – a shift in emphasis was clearly required, and Smith wasted no time. For those who had perceived the manager as being a cautious individual, his foray into the transfer market offered a pleasant surprise. The first, most important, piece of business was completed when Andy Goram was acquired from Hibernian for £1m, and Smith snapped up David Robertson from Aberdeen and Stuart McCall from Everton. As the revolving door whirled, Trevor Steven, Terry Hurlock and Nigel Spackman exited, and Alexei

Mikhailichenko and Dale Gordon entered. Smith's attitude was that he saw players he valued, he offered them terms and a deal was negotiated if these were mutually acceptable. No fuss. Smith and Knox also spelled out the message that the reserve team had to be viewed as a priority, considering the urgency of developing young Scots into first-team performers. The boss also insisted that oil paintings of eight predecessors – William Winton, Bill Struth, Scot Symon, Davie White, Willie Waddell, Jock Wallace, John Greig and Graeme Souness – should be hung in his oak-panelled office. 'They were scattered all over the stadium, and I thought it would be nice to have them all hanging together to remind me of the men who had shaped the club's history from the very early days. Was it intimidating? Naw. It was inspiring, more like.'

The recruitment of Goram was a shrewd move. The gifted goalkeeper had proved repeatedly that he was of international class during his travails at cash-strapped Hibs. Though never far from controversy before or after his arrival at Ibrox, or in subsequent years when his name became a common feature on the front and back pages of the tabloids, Goram provided the dependable last line in an already robust defence. Smith was also bolstered by a resurgent Ally McCoist, who had been one of the beneficiaries of Souness's return to Anfield. From being stuck on the bench so often that he was nicknamed The Judge, the striker was informed by Smith before the league kick-off that he would be a pivotal member of the starting line-up every week. That news was the catalyst for McCoist to contribute a flurry of opportunistic goals, and beaming smiles, which tantalised opponents. He was the very devil to contain when he was in his element, yet any individual inclined to dismiss him as a cheeky Jack-the-lad with a superficial gloss would discover in his company that he is a thoughtful individual, and he was genuinely undermined by being forced to languish on the periphery at Ibrox. It is hardly surprising that McCoist should wax lyrical about the manner in which he was offered redemption by his mentor Smith. He told me:

'Walter knows a lot about football, but he also knows an awful lot about what makes human beings tick, and I was eternally grateful to him for bringing me back into the fold, because no footballer likes being sidelined, and I was as frustrated as the next man. As it was, life at Ibrox under Walter was one of the most enjoyable periods of my life. Sure, it helped that we won trophies and were generally successful, but there was much more to it than that: he fostered a shared purpose among all the guys, he knew when to shout and when to crack a joke, and it was brilliant going into the ground every morning and knowing that we were all joining forces again.

'Nothing beats it. Nothing. That sensation of waking up on Saturdays and getting myself psyched up for three o'clock – and the banter, the ribbing and the wind-ups which are part and parcel of the daily training routines – and then hearing the mighty roar when you step out of the dressing room.

'At Rangers, under Walter, everybody was pulling in the one direction, and you forge bonds which are never broken when you live like that with a group of people for any length of time. Yes it was hard, we were constantly under pressure to perform at a high level, and the gaffer was spot-on when he remarked that you are never more than two defeats away from a crisis at Ibrox. But he was a fantastic motivator, partly because he had so much passion for the club that it filtered down to everybody else, even the guys who joined us from abroad, who might only have a fleeting knowledge of Rangers.'

Some difficult adjustments were required as Smith fine-tuned his new squad, not least because of another continental disappointment for the club. The basic format of the European Cup had been altered, with the last eight being formed into two groups of four, as UEFA gradually advanced towards the creation of the Champions League. There seemed no reason for Rangers to be fearful when they were pitted against Sparta Prague in the first round, though the collapse of communist regimes had sparked a surge in nationalistic fervour throughout those countries that were no longer under the yoke. They were drawn away in the first leg, and a considerable number of supporters travelled to the old Eastern Bloc confident that their team could only improve on their display a decade earlier, when they had been trounced 3-0 by Dukla Prague. Their optimism proved ill-founded as Rangers served up a stuttering showing, which exposed them at regular intervals. The Scots were mighty fortunate to be only 1-0 down at the end, the goal arriving courtesy of Jiri Nemec's dipping cross, which unusually was misjudged by the despairing Goram. On another night with a different referee, Rangers could have conceded two or three penalties for a string of rash challenges as they fought to stem the tide, but despite the wretched nature of the performance, they were probably still entitled to regard themselves as favourites in the home leg. Once again early promise, passion and pace that promoted a swirl of noise from the stands at Ibrox came to naught. Rangers had moved into the lead in the tie with two goals from McCall, and were obliged only to maintain their discipline and shape, but the Czechs, deservedly over the two games, were gifted victory deep in extra time when Goram fumbled a deflected Horst Siegl back-heel. It was an inauspicious European baptism for the new keeper, but The Goalie would more than atone for the blunders in months and years ahead. Not that that offered him, or Smith, any consolation in the immediate aftermath.

The manager now had to concentrate on preserving domestic supremacy and striving for new levels of consistency, plus satisfying rising numbers of supporters cramming into Ibrox. Critics of the Souness regime might suggest that Rangers simply bought success, but that policy has never stopped people joining the crowd when it works, and Smith's job proved to be a delicate balance between eking out victories against teams who came to Glasgow in search of a draw, and serving up entertaining football whatever the negative tactics of the opposition. Rangers were not always successful, but statistics tell a stirring tale: in 1986–7 the average attendance was just over 20,000, by 1988 it had advanced to 30,000, and as the club progressed into the 1990s the figure had risen beyond 40,000. Even if one accepts that many of these spectators were formerly disillusioned fans or fair-weather friends, the crowds remain a testimony to the zeal with which Smith propelled his team forward. He was growing used to dealing in the multi-million-pound transfer market, a process for which life at Dundee United had left him ill-equipped. This was one of the domains where Smith, as a pragmatic, hard-headed operator, was occasionally left floundering by some sharp-suited agents, who could talk a better game than some of their clients played it. Yet the manager persuaded some truly international class talent to journey to Ibrox, and if he was guilty of the occasional mistake, no boss is faultless when it comes to hiring and firing staff. His signing philosophy, alluded to previously, was based on four tenets: Will the player be good for Rangers on the pitch? Will he generate positive vibes in the dressing room? Will I have to spend an excessive amount of time worrying about what the player is up to when he isn't at Ibrox? Can I rely on this player to dig me out of a hole when the going gets tough, as undoubtedly it will, at certain times during the campaign? These priorities might have differed in their order, according to whether x or y was coming from within Scotland or abroad, but they exemplified the message that Smith was not looking for strutting showmen who would respond to the adulation of a packed Ibrox with feats of trickery and sleight-of-foot. He required footballers to exude the same level of commitment and desire on mid-week games played out in miserable wintry conditions, whether at East End Park, Broomfield or elsewhere.

It was evident that few would offer any sympathy if he messed up, and given the residual bitterness which supporters of other clubs harboured towards the Old Firm, he approached his task with a single-mindedness that was passed on to his foot soldiers, ensuring a scorched-earth policy in the sporting sense for the next two seasons. Rangers opened their 1991–2 league itinerary with a 6-0 rout of St Johnstone, Mark Hateley collecting a hat-trick.

He added another two as Celtic were brushed aside 2-0: the disparate parts of Smith's ensemble were knitting together. As the weeks passed, the massed ranks of Rangers fans lapped up the familiar sight of McCoist hurtling away from another stricken defence, arms aloft in jubilation, while on the other side of the Old Firm, the efforts of the Celtic board to extricate themselves from a financial mire merely deepened the sense of gloom among their support. Rangers continued with a remorseless surge. Aberdeen, who remained a threat, were defeated 3-2 at Pittodrie in December as the prelude to Celtic being overcome by 3-1 at New Year, and even when Hearts sought to initiate some sort of sustained title challenge, the ubiquitous McCoist snuffed out their hopes with the only goal of the game at Tynecastle in February. Generally it was as comprehensive an exhibition of collective responsibility as could have been requested, and while Smith was determined to downplay his achievements and refused to get carried away by it all, he privately acknowledged that his side had reacted pretty well to his insistence on 90-minute displays.

For neutrals some of these displays were a joy to behold, but impartial souls tend to be thin on the ground in the west of Scotland, in particular, and it was around the start of 1992 that Celtic fans started seriously to peddle the conviction that Rangers were nothing more than an efficient bunch of hired assassins, and that they could not be compared in any way with the Lisbon Lions and the vintage of the late 1960s and early '70s, who had won nine consecutive titles. It was as if some of these individuals could not foresee a quick end to their suffering, and were therefore intent on stressing that Celtic had embarked on their trophy gathering with a clutch of Scots who were born within a limited geographical radius. Smith gave this argument short shrift. He would confess to feeling admiration for that earlier Celtic side, but he would make no apologies for hiring the people that he believed were best for his purposes, and anyway it was futile to indulge in comparisons between teams of different generations. What could be deduced was that any Old Firm side would have benefited from a strike partnership such as Hateley and McCoist, but though most of my Celtic-supporting colleagues were generous enough to grant that Rangers had taken strides forward from the rather sterile showings that were commonplace under Souness's stewardship, they stuck to the view that the only true test of the Ibrox club's credentials would be if Celtic were capable of launching a riposte.

On the run-in to a fourth league championship in succession, which had amounted to little more than a procession, Smith and his men greeted St Mirren at Ibrox on 19 April in the knowledge that victory would seal the prize. It was typical of Rangers that they offered a stirring exhibition with no shortage of skill. McCoist, as unquenchable as he had been for the rest of the campaign, opened the scoring early on, and as the visitors' ramparts were increasingly battered, second-half goals from Gary Stevens, McCoist and Pieter Huistra wrapped up the title. More than 40,000 of the faithful hailed the old-stagers and the new-comers, and sang themselves hoarse as Smith waved to all parts of the stadium. In the final analysis, they posted all kind of mile-stones during a season of rampant achievement. They scored more than a century of goals for the first time since 1939, and lost just five matches in 44 fixtures: if the current structure had been in place with three points for a win, Rangers would have amassed 105 points. McCoist, perhaps inevitably, was the leading marks-man with 34 goals, every one a reminder of Graeme Souness's faulty judgment, but also a tribute to the striker's ability to bounce back from adversity.

Nor was there any slackening of the Rangers' commitment when they ran on to the pitch at Hampden Park for the Scottish Cup final against Airdrie on 10 May. Much had been made in advance of their poor record in this competition, and how they had flattered to deceive even in the Souness years. Smith noted patiently the stream of largely tabloid-inspired fodder, which was designed to whip up interest in a match that might otherwise have looked less than a contest, but he did admit that his side's Scottish

Cup form had been fairly unimpressive. On the only previous occasion in which he had been involved in a final, Celtic's Joe Miller had secured the trophy in 1989, and Rangers had experienced embarrassment against Hamilton and Dunfermline, so some observers wondered if pawky, industrious Airdrie might just inflict a fresh surprise on their famous opponents. Smith told the press it was a game in which his team had to score first. As had been the case for much of the season, he gained his wish when Hateley opened the account after half-an-hour, then McCoist struck on the edge on the interval to deflate the underdogs. The Airdrie players rolled up their sleeves and pulled a goal back through Andy Smith, which precipitated a fraught climax, but Rangers held on to attain their first league and cup double for 14 years. All this had been immensely rewarding for Smith, but in lifting a glass of wine to toast the twin achievements, thoughts would be turned to the future, and especially that thorny issue of European competition.

CHAPTER NINE

AMAZING ADVENTURES IN EUROPE

❖

'Let's fire this in, and see what happens'

There is no other way to describe the 1992–3 season for Rangers except in the language of victory and triumph. Heady performances were enacted in front of packed crowds, who rose to acclaim a sequence of redoubtable team displays and outstanding individual exploits that were imbued with a sense that anything was possible. It was gallus, to use a distinctly Scottish description; it was Glaswegian swagger, and the campaign twisted and turned in unexpected directions. Indeed Rangers might well have triumphed in the European Cup, but for enough corruption and underhand behaviour from opponents to delight conspiracy theorists. It was unquestionably one of the club's greatest seasons, overseen by a man apparently endowed with a doctorate in football alchemy. That certainly seems to be the feeling of several of those who appeared in the treble-winning year. Trevor Steven, who had returned to Ibrox from Olympique Marseille, summed up the mood around the camp:

'Everything just clicked, and there was this shared feeling that we could go out and offer anybody in Europe a decent match. It wasn't over-confidence, but Walter Smith had done a magnificent job in building up team morale and getting the boys to pull together, and everything went well – the training sessions, the pre-season, the nights out, the works – so that we were as fit as we had ever been, and of course the lads had built up so much momentum as the previous year had progressed that it was like pressing a switch when Walter sent us out for battle again. We weren't taking anything for granted, but he made us confident, we all knew our jobs, what we were supposed to be doing, and were all fighting fit. You can't underestimate the buzz which goes through a dressing room when that happens.'

Another of the team told me that Smith assembled the Rangers squad at an opulent hotel away from Glasgow, and methodically conveyed his wishes and plans in advance of the Scottish league schedule.

'He relayed the message to us that we had to be utterly ruthless and focus on nothing else but giving 100 per cent for Rangers, and that if we did that, he would stand by us all. He told us that the league was still extremely important and that our supporters wouldn't tolerate us becoming sidetracked by Europe, but it was clear the latter was very, very important to him. I heard that he had met with [David] Murray, and that the chairman had promised Walter significant amounts of cash if the Champions League went well for the club. So he was making it clear to us that we had to be ultra-professional in every match, that we hadn't done ourselves justice in Europe in the last two years, and that it was time to set the record straight and show we could go where Aberdeen had gone [in winning the European Cup-Winners' Cup]. He really hammered home that point, that if a club of Aberdeen's stature could beat Real Madrid and enjoy such a marvellous success in that company, that there was no reason for Rangers to be apprehensive about tackling anybody, if we showed the right attitude and had the belief in our own abilities. It was a pretty inspiring speech. Walter sometimes gets described as a bit dour and down-in-the-mouth, but when he was talking to us that day his eyes were sparkling, he was animated about the challenges ahead, and it was riveting stuff. We went away thinking: "Well, if the gaffer reckons that we have the potential to lift the European Cup, why don't we prove him right?" '

Having scrutinised the players at his disposal, Smith was amply justified in his optimism. McCoist and Hateley had already knitted together superbly during their alliance, and had demonstrated their avaricious appetite for goals, and the presence in midfield of such stalwarts as Ian Durrant, Trevor Steven, Ian Ferguson and John Brown meant that Rangers would be nobody's pushovers. Add the likes of Richard Gough, Dave McPherson, Andy Goram, Steven Pressley, Pieter Huistra and Gary McSwegan to the mix, and they made up an ensemble that would probably have beaten the Scotland side in 1992–3. They were too strong for any of their club opponents as the weeks and months passed, and what had always threatened to be a one-sided championship quickly turned into a stroll in the park. True, Rangers were tested during a 1-1 draw with Celtic at Ibrox in August, an outcome which persuaded some of the more optimistic Hoops followers to proclaim that their side could launch a sustained title fight, but Rangers embarked on an unbeaten sequence of the type that drives opponents to distraction. It extended for seven months and encapsulated a total of 44 matches in all competitions, and featured myriad instances of striking trickery from McCoist and Hateley, encouraging even the most cautious of Ibrox fans to acknowledge that their team were something special.

The league was wrapped up efficiently, the battle more or less won, when Rangers, who had already moved five points clear of Aberdeen, travelled to Pittodrie and emerged with a 1-0 victory. The climax came on 2 May 1993, in the unprepossessing setting of Broomfield Park, where Airdrie attempted vainly to halt the blue juggernaut. Smith had lost the services of his talisman McCoist, who had suffered a broken leg, and it was left to deputy McSwegan to score the only goal of the afternoon after 46 minutes in an encounter characterised by numerous scoring opportunities for the visitors, which were not accepted. If that profligacy annoyed the manager, the fact remained that Rangers had accrued 97 goals in 44 league matches, 34 springing from McCoist. The Dons finished second in the table on 64 points to the champions' 73.

Domestic cup competitions brought similar exhibitions of clinical professionalism and hungry execution. In the League Cup dénouement on 25 October 1992, Smith's men arrived at the stand-in venue of Celtic Park feeling the strain of a midweek meeting in Europe with Leeds United, and were soon locked in a thrilling tussle with Aberdeen, which marked the fourth occasion in six years in which the clubs had met in the final. It had promised to be a tense affair considering the fractious history between the teams, and once again Smith asked for an early goal, Stuart McCall obliging in 14 minutes after Theo Snelders was involved in a mix-up with David Winnie. The setback did not faze the men from Pittodrie, and as the contest ebbed and flowed, Duncan Shearer levelled the score in the second half to force extra-time. Smith confessed that he had been worried – 'The concern for us was how the players would be able to cope with another 30 minutes after their exertions against Leeds' – but befitting the discipline, control and relentless energy which had become their trademark, Rangers dominated the match the longer it progressed, and eventually defender Gary Smith put the ball into his own net when under pressure from Hateley. The victors looked as fresh at the end as if it was their second or third match of the campaign . . . such was the conviction and camaraderie beating in the heart of this side.

The Scottish Cup offered the inevitability of Rangers again locking horns with Aberdeen, and ultimately prevailing, though they had to surmount various obstacles before the trophy was secured. Sceptics might glance at their cup-ties, which were all away from home, and suggest that they had it easy. Once they had disposed of Motherwell, they might have faced sterner adversaries than Ayr United and Arbroath, but in the semi-final versus Hearts, Rangers fell behind to an Allan Preston goal scored on the hour, and for a spell seemed to be struggling to regain the initiative against fired-up opponents. 'It was one of those afternoons where you just have to keep battling away and getting the basics right, because Hearts performed well and they had reached a number of semis and finals in the previous few years only to come a cropper, so they were really desperate to make this count,' recalls Scott Nisbet, one of the unsung stalwarts of Rangers' success. As the atmosphere intensified and the Edinburgh club strove to exorcise the spectre of past disappointments, they were stunned when Dave McPherson, who had been one of their own in the previous season, produced the equaliser as the prelude to McCoist dashing Hearts' aspirations with a late winner. It was a familiar scenario. Frequently Rangers would find themselves under the cosh or struggling to find their rhythm, then one of their number, be it McCoist, Durrant or Trevor Steven, would orchestrate a piece of magic while the defence harassed adversaries out of their stride, even if it meant dwelling on the margins of legality. The statistics could not be faulted – the team's goal difference of plus-62 required no addendum – and the trust which built up among the players cemented the notion that any situation was retrievable. 'The pride the boys took in the jersey was incredible,' Smith observed. David Murray also marvelled at the transformation which had been implemented since the departure of Graeme Souness. Now for sure Rangers were still combative, but without the malice aforethought that had characterised the Souness-managed team. 'Everybody played hard for each other, and that pulled us through,' Murray declared. That assessment succinctly epitomised the qualities which underpinned the team's other outstanding achievements.

By the time they made the short journey to Parkhead for the Scottish Cup final on 29 May 1993, the Rangers team could have been forgiven for having one eye on their holiday destinations. If they were not quite at their peak on the day, Smith's tactical nous ensured that youthful precocity had a starring role in the match: forced into switching his line-up because of the long-term injury to McCoist, he called up Neil Murray for the biggest experience of his life, and the youngster unleashed a ferocious long-range drive which opened the scoring in the 22nd minute. It was one of those episodes where a footballing hunch is regarded as inspired, and as the Rangers hordes celebrated in anticipation of a treble, Mark Hateley doubled the advantage. Aberdeen, who had slogged their guts out all season without tangible reward, were deflated by ending as runners-up in all three domestic competitions, and their so-called consolation goal through Lee Richardson was nothing of the sort. 'Credit to them, they had snapped at our heels in the league and clung on determinedly in the cups,' Smith said afterwards, as he gazed around Celtic Park wondering whether there would be this number of jubilant Rangers fans inside the stadium ever again. But it was a fitting finale to what had been a tremendous feat by his squad, the only bone of contention what might have been, or perhaps should have been, in the European Cup.

❖

If this account had been written in strict chronological order, Rangers' foreign adventures would have slipped in and out of the narrative, and clarity would have been obscured. Hence the decision to concentrate at length on the Ibrox club's protracted and devilishly-near flirtation with the prize that had eluded Scotland's representatives since the 1960s. The first-round tie against Lyngby of Denmark saw the Scots ease through as 3-0 aggregate winners, with goals from Mark Hateley and Pieter Huistra in Glasgow and Ian Durrant at the Parkenstadion. Such an outcome was expected, but thereafter Smith enjoyed a string of superb results against some formidable teams, starting with the second-round tussle against Leeds United. As usual with these affairs the cliché 'Battle of Britain' was rolled out, but even by the standards of hyperbole surrounding previous clashes of teams from north and south of the Border, this encounter provoked a torrent of comment, analysis and patriotic hogwash. Leeds had advanced to this stage of the tournament after being reinstated by UEFA following a breach of the nationality regulations by Stuttgart, who had beaten them on goal difference before the outcome was reversed, and Leeds won a one-off third match by 2-1. Then there was the contrast in the managers' personalities. Smith, an introverted figure at press conferences, was tagged by the English press as living up to PG Wodehouse's maxim: 'It is never difficult to distinguish between a Scotsman with a grievance and a ray of sunshine.' By comparison, his Leeds' counterpart Howard Wilkinson was one of the bright young things of the English circuit, who was tipped to take charge of the national team in the future. It was also a compelling tie considering that Rangers' achievements since the late 1980s were derided in England as owing more to the deficiencies of opponents than to genuine qualities. The English media asserted that when United travelled to Glasgow for the first leg equipped with such inter-national-class performers as Eric Cantona, Gary McAllister and Gordon Strachan, they would soon highlight the paucity of Scottish football talent by sweeping past their rivals.

That verdict seemed justified when McAllister dispatched a brilliant 20-yard strike past the despairing Goram. Gloomy home followers, though, should have known that their heroes were as resilient as they were committed, and despite an opening spell when the likes of Cantona swanned around the Ibrox turf, the hosts regrouped and mounted their own attacks, and gradually the tide turned in their favour. It helped that Goram was the personification of solidity and poise in his goals whereas Leeds' John Lukic looked uncomfortable in pursuing crosses, and a succession of Rangers corners finished with Lukic punching the ball into his own net. A mere quarter of the way through the match the visitors' swagger had been made to evaporate, and it was no shock when another treacherous Durrant corner was met by McPherson for Lukic to parry the ball to McCoist, who seized the opportunity with the glee. I spoke to several Rangers supporters in the days that followed, and they were convinced that Smith had been too negative in not pressing for a third goal. When I sought to counter this with the opinion that they needed only a draw at Elland Road, whereas the balance would have been different if Leeds had snatched a 2-2 draw, their scornful countenances reflected one of the less appealing aspects of the Rangers brethren. Namely, their refusal to accept that Smith, an individual with 15 years of coaching experience under his belt, might just know his job better than they did. Fans are entitled to grow agitated when their team slump regularly, but this was the Ibrox men on the hottest of streaks, and still grumbling could be discerned. No wonder that one player involved in that Rangers victory told me (on strict condition that he remained anonymous): 'Most of our support are terrific, but there are some wee guys out there with a bag of chips on both shoulders, who have never forgiven their father for being only five foot six. When you're sitting on the bench, you can hear them screaming stuff like: "That was f***ing shite, McCoist. You are a disgrace to Rangers." And you just feel like walking up to them and saying: "Do you know that we are actually winning 3-0, you wee prick!" But you can't argue with these folk. We could be beating Celtic 6-2, and they would still be moaning that our defence was a shambles. Sometimes it's hard to take, but you just have to remember that for every little tube like him, there are a hundred other decent people who respond fantastically every Saturday.'

Even the most hard-to-please Rangers spectators must have been enraptured in the early stages of the return leg when Hateley, showing marvellous agility and precision, volleyed spectacularly past Lukic from at least 25 yards. In an instant Leeds United were transformed into a panic-stricken rabble. They piled on waves of pressure that was not particularly inspiring, and a group of their supporters were heard screaming abuse, but Goram remained in imperious form, and Richard Gough slowed the pace as if to rile watching Tykes even more. Rangers established a stranglehold which was reinforced when Durrant and Hateley conjured up a glorious sweeping move, from which McCoist's header sealed victory. Nothing could have been sweeter for Smith and his players than to overcome the English on their own territory, though Cantona scored towards the end. It was noticeable that the majority of the losing fans accorded Rangers a standing ovation, in acknowledgement of the quality football that they had exhibited.

Smith refused to gloat over the defeat of Leeds, preferring to concentrate on the European Cup's revamped format in which the last eight were divided into two groups of four, the winners of each section progressing to the final. Nowadays it seems an antiquated structure, but at least the Champions League did not break the trade descriptions act in that period by granting entry to clubs who had finished second or third in their championships. Rangers were drawn in a group with Club Brugge, CSKA Moscow and Olympique Marseille, which would mean testing examinations for their mettle, but the prospect was not too daunting from the Ibrox perspective. On the contrary, Smith maintained his calm exterior when confronted with a series of problems, including injuries and suspension to key players such as McCoist and Ian Ferguson, and despite being restricted in his options by UEFA's non-national policy. He prepared for the opening match versus Marseille in Glasgow on 25 November 1992, by fielding the callow triumvirate of Neil Murray, Steven Pressley and Gary McSwegan, who were asked to make their European debuts against the might of the French title-holders, who had reached the European final two years earlier. Smith's plans were undermined when his captain Richard Gough departed after 45 minutes with a knock, but Rangers clung on during a putrid winter's evening, though the visitors had threatened to run riot. Alen Boksic and Rudi Voller had handed Marseille a comfortable two-goal cushion, or so it appeared, but substitute McSwegan suddenly reduced the deficit with a stunning header, which just happened to be his first touch of the game and his maiden competitive goal for Rangers. For the home crowd, who had been silenced gradually by the appalling weather combined with the patent superiority of the Frenchmen, it was the cue to erupt into a clamour for an old-fashioned, roll-your-sleeves-up climax, so beloved by Scottish football worthies. It helped to do the trick. In the 81st minute, Hateley headed the ball home from a Durrant cross, and the faint prospect arose of Rangers snatching the unlikeliest of victories, when even their most biased fans would surely have admitted that they had been overwhelmed for three-quarters of the affair. In the event they had to be content with a 2-2 result, but the reaction of Smith and Archie Knox was that of men who had grown up watching *The Great Escape*, and who were delighted to have been involved in a football version of the movie. They realised that Rangers had to improve by several notches in subsequent fixtures if they were not to suffer an ignominious exit from the competition.

In gauging the company that Rangers were keeping, the next tussle was against CSKA Moscow, who had qualified for the group stages with a superb triumph over cup-holders Barcelona, rallying from losing 2-0 at the Nou Camp to eliminating the Spanish team by 3-2. Because of the ferocious nature of the Russian winter, the Muscovites were forced to stage their home matches in Germany, and they constituted a formidable threat when Smith and his compatriots made for the imposing Ruhrstadion on December 9 accompanied by more than 8,000 fans. The supporters had begun to imagine that if Rangers could keep using their get-out-of-jail card as astutely as had been manifest against Marseille, then almost anything was possible. A galvanised Rangers team grabbed the lead within 13 minutes via Ian Durrant, and were the epitome of professionalism for the remainder of the tie, limiting their opponents' chances and demonstrating the scale of the improvement made under Smith.

That marked a three-month break for the Champions League during which the Scots continued to reign majestically over domestic rivals. The March resumption of European action brought a double-header with Brugge, which on paper seemed to offer the best hopes of points. On their crusade to Belgium's Olympiastadion Rangers were near the height of their powers, consistently troubling their adversaries. Despite falling behind to a Tomasz Dziubinski goal on the stroke of the interval, they assumed control of the midfield and gained the ascendancy throughout the second half, Pieter Huistra equalising in the 73rd minute for a share of the spoils. Thus the re-match assumed an increasing degree of importance, and what a spectacle it was! I can recall a nagging feeling that Rangers would come a cropper when they were cast as favourites, and Smith gave warning that the Belgians would be dangerous: he had been impressed with their quality during the first meeting. It seemed that he need not have worried, for the prolific Durrant broke the deadlock in the 39th minute of another rain-lashed evening in Glasgow. Scottish teams, though, rarely participate in such must-win encounters without introducing crises, and Rangers' fortunes suffered when Hateley was sent off in controversial circumstances, then Lorenzo Staelens levelled the match early in the second period. Smith appreciated that a draw was no use, and urged his men further forward. It was a risky policy that might have cost him dear on another evening, but not this one. Scott Nisbet's clinching goal is etched in the memory: it was a startling score, a slo-mo in real time that baffled a Brugge defence who probably still suffer nightmares about it. From wide on the right, Nisbet struck a swerving shot-cum-cross which took a wicked bounce to fly at a devilish angle past the bemused Danny Verlinden and into the net. Many have dismissed it as a fluke, but Nisbet – whose career was cruelly cut short three days later after he sustained an injury at Celtic Park – told me otherwise:

'Let's face it, in these conditions with the rain pouring down and the wind howling, the most important thing was to keep troubling their goalkeeper, and when I ran forward I thought to myself: "Let's fire this in, and see what happens." To that extent I suppose it was a speculative effort, but it wasn't just a hit and hope, as some have alleged. I was aiming at the goal, and although I couldn't have imagined that the ball would move as it did, it was the kind of evening when something like that was always liable to happen, and I am just glad that it worked in our favour, not against us, and we ended up getting the victory which we needed.'

If luck seemed to be favouring the Scots, their optimism was soon checked. On the evening that Nisbet attained his priceless goal, Marseille trounced CSKA Moscow 6-0, and suspicions began to circulate that the French club's voluble owner Bernard Tapie was determined that the Champions League would be won by his team, and that he was not especially bothered how that was achieved. His side were probably the most talented in the tournament, but resentment increased as the group moved towards its climax, and for Rangers the next few weeks turned into a classic tale of what might have been. When they ventured to the Stade Velodrome, they had already been angered by their opponents' underhand approach to providing tickets for travelling fans – only 1,000 were made available, breaching an agreement that 4,000 would be on offer – but that merely acted as an impetus. Rangers were far more convincing than they had been in tackling Marseille at home, even if the absence of the suspended Hateley ultimately proved costly. With one of his main strikers out of contention, Smith plumped for the emerging McSwegan, but the reality was that the manager needed all his luminaries when facing a team of the calibre of Marseille in their cauldron-like amphitheatre. The visitors did recover from ceding a goal after David Robertson's carelessness had allowed Franck Sauzee to score in the first half; Durrant equalised in another testimony to his perseverance. The French team might have secured victory on several occasions, but there again McSwegan, a replacement for Huistra, saw a scything shot flash narrowly wide. It was fast and riveting, but 1-1 was but a moral victory for the Scots, who now had to trust that they could beat CSKA Moscow at Ibrox, and hope Brugge could do them a favour against Marseille. But fair play took a beating in the build-up to these fixtures in what had proved to be a captivating group. Rangers' historian Robert McElroy noted that sufficient bad blood existed between Brugge and their French rivals for the Scots to be optimistic that Tapie's club would face a stern examination when they travelled to Belgium:

'Both the club and their fans felt that they had been badly treated at the Stade Velodrome on match-day two. The visiting supporters had been the subject of shocking abuse from the Marseille crowd, whilst home coach Raymond Goethals had insulted the opposition with disparaging remarks about Brugge following his side's 3-0 win. The Belgians had sworn revenge, promising that they would defeat Marseille at their home ground, where they had remained unbeaten for so long, and had made that very promise to Rangers following the two matches between the clubs in March: "Keep the group alive until match-day six, and we will defeat the French for you." The group was indeed still alive, but something had changed in the last few days. The Belgians had sworn that they would avenge their honour, yet on the eve of battle they mysteriously changed their tune. Three key players were supposedly injured, the next weekend's league match was now considered more important, and Brugge meekly surrendered a home record of which they were extremely proud, going down to an early Boksic goal after just two minutes. Meanwhile at Ibrox intense home pressure [against CSKA] failed to achieve a breakthrough, perhaps a dozen good chances being squandered, with again the absent Hateley being sorely missed by Rangers.'

The dream was over, but Rangers' misgivings and regrets were wholly justified, for reports subsequently emerged of Tapie's involvement in bribery and corruption. The controversial official was sentenced to four years' imprisonment, his club were relegated and stripped of the championship that they had won that season, and it remains a mystery why UEFA did not step into the affair with their own investigation of Marseille's conduct in the Champions League. Among the damning evidence against Tapie was a list of matches which the president had bribed opponents to throw, and prominent on this roster was their game in Brugge, which had proved so damaging to Rangers' prospects of reaching the final (in which Marseille beat AC Milan 1-0 thanks to a Basile Boli goal). Smith and David Murray refused to indulge in public breast-beating, but the bottom line is that Marseille had acted illegally and lost their French title in the process, and the logical extension would have been for UEFA to strip them of their Champions League prize, and to charge them with bringing the game into disrepute.

It had proved to be a watershed season for Rangers none-theless, in that they had gone 10 games unbeaten in Europe's premier competition. They managed that feat despite a fixture schedule which obliged players to participate in 64 matches for their club, and the majority of their leading lights were also involved in international duty. It was a gruelling regime for squad members and the management team, which possibly explains why Smith chose to speak out about the ridiculous workload heaped on his personnel rather than be dragged into a debate about the French judicial system. He stressed his apprehension about the future if the SFA and SFL did not recognise that it was not viable to engage in 44 league fixtures every season, and though the domestic structure was overhauled 18 months later, that did not help Rangers as they attempted to fly the flag for Scotland single-handedly on the European beat. From Smith's perspective in 1992–3, the principal weakness of the Scottish structure was its sheer inflexibility and the fashion in which the intense routine sapped the stamina and creativity of even the most talented and enthusiastic youngsters:

'Club managers have been preaching this message for years – that the number of games should be reduced, and that players should have fewer matches in midweek. That allows time for all of us to work with the players, and also allows them necessary recovery time in between games. That's time to have injuries treated, time to rest if that is what is necessary, time to hone their skills and to work on any part of their game which needs developing. But in my spell in charge at Rangers there has been no time for any of that. All we have been able to do with the players is try to maintain their fitness level during the season, and try to allow them time to shake off the nagging injuries which come with the general wear and tear that these heavy domestic programmes bring in their wake. During the Champions League run we even had to resort to taking the players for a walk and finishing up in a transport café for coffee and bacon rolls, because to work them any harder would simply have been counter-productive. But is that really what we want to be doing in the long term? Of course not, but we can't change it. The authorities have to change it.'

Despite the strength of his argument, Smith's views attracted scant support, which was a measure of the rather depressing antipathy which was felt towards Rangers at the time. The trouble was that though they had attained some of the success they coveted in Europe, their performances owed more to team spirit and strength of character than to free-flowing, adventurous football. But then many Scottish fans seemed to assume that they could saunter on to the field against the likes of Leeds and Marseille and indulge in 100mph, hell-for-leather action. It perhaps summed up the gulf between fact and fiction that some Scottish newspapers, *Scotland on Sunday* included, attempted to draw comparisons between Jock Stein's 1967 Lisbon Lions and Smith's 1993 Champions League squad, when it should have been obvious that Stein's side sprang from a wholly different culture. In that era tanner-ba' exponents such as Jimmy Johnstone had licence to spark mayhem in opposition ranks, and most defenders could do only one thing, namely defend. The Celtic team who triumphed in the European Cup fully merit their prodigious renown, and Johnstone was a wondrous sprite with a magician's expertise, but that does not mean that followers of the game should be dismissive of a Rangers squad who served up thrills of their own, even if these diminished as the Champions League intensity mounted and the emphasis was less on exciting audiences than on playing the percentages. Smith himself acknowledged that his team had limitations. They were more reliant on Hateley than should have been a side with genuine European aspirations; McCoist glittered in the early European ties, but went off the boil the longer the competition rumbled on. He suffered a fractured leg shortly after Rangers' elimination, which added to the injuries, strains and assorted niggles which had accumulated as 10 matches became 20, then 40, then 50 and more. Some of the stars were dead on their feet, and others could barely stand.

The disappointing nature of the conclusion to Rangers' European campaign should not be permitted to disguise the scale of their exploits. Only two years previously, Graeme Souness had lamented that he would never achieve anything on the Continent when restricted to 11 Scots, but here we had a predominantly home-grown team packed with redoubtable figures such as McCoist, McCall, Goram, Brown, Ferguson, Durrant and Gough, who did club and country proud in a volatile environment. If there was a problem, it lay in the fact that Europe nagged away at Smith and Murray like the toothache. They appreciated that their supporters were desperate for as many domestic prizes as could be accumulated, but as the manager countered, what was the point of reigning supreme at home if that could not be translated into tangible rewards outwith the country? Unfortunately, as subsequent events emphasised, there were several reasons for the prognosis that this Rangers squad had gone as far as they could without major surgery, and that future signings would have to involve sophisticated and versatile performers who could grace the grand stadiums of Europe. Which made all the more mystifying the club's summer investment in 1993, which was more or less limited to the purchase of the gangly and scowling Duncan Ferguson from Dundee United for £3.75m, which was, and still is, an astonishing figure. But then managers are not permitted the benefit of hindsight in these transactions, and football history is littered with stories of men who were proclaimed as superstars in the making and initially applauded by the fans, but who turned out to be anything but super.

It would be remiss, however, to conclude an appreciation of the heroics of 1992–3 on a sour note. Instead, I recall watching Walter Smith on the periphery of the action as Rangers battered away at CSKA Moscow without being able to pierce their resistance. Afterwards a friend of mine named Ally Scott, who had no allegiance to the Ibrox club beyond wishing all Scottish teams success in Europe, faxed me from Germany, where he was based, with the message: 'Hi there, just watched the Gers go out of the Champions League, but not without giving 100 per cent effort and going so close that I actually feel a bit sad tonight. You look back on the tournament and think that Hateley shouldn't have been sent off against Brugge. And if he had been available in these last two matches [against Marseille and CSKA] I would have put money on him scoring at least two of the chances which were missed by other people. So near and so far. But they have gone through the competition without losing, and that is one hell of an achievement. Here's to 94!' Maybe hard-luck stories are too frequent in Scottish sport, but in the final analysis Smith's demeanour throughout that Champions League foray was symbolic of the man. On occasion he quietly bemoaned losing Hateley to suspension while launching into a reasoned debate on the best way forward for Scottish clubs, as the major European tournament developed into a schism between the haves and have-nots. But for the most part, he seemed thrilled to be pitting his brains and his blackboard against the best coaches from the rest of the Continent. The problem was that once you have won a treble and reached the equivalent of the semi-finals of the European Cup, where else is there to go? It was a question which would induce much head-scratching and soul-searching for Smith, Archie Knox and David Murray.

CHAPTER TEN

PAPERING OVER THE CRACKS

❖

*'Smith had discovered yet again how fickle
the soccer public can be'*

Walter Smith is usually portrayed as a phlegmatic character, a stoical man in the face of adversity, and he required these qualities in abundance when the euphoria of the treble-winning season had passed, and he was forced to endure a string of travails as Rangers, without any great success, attempted to crank up the momentum generated by their exploits in the Champions League. Such achievements served the manager well, as it was easier to attract high-calibre players to Ibrox with the incentive of appearing in several European ties in each campaign. On the debit side, he discovered that the tremendous team spirit that he had established within the ranks was not easy to replicate after signing new personnel, especially when negative stories started seeping into the press. As a hard-nosed newspaper reader since his youth, Smith knew the score with the tabloids, so if one of his men was caught over-indulging in alcohol or in a melee at a taxi rank, he realised that the ensuing publicity would hardly be pleasant, but it would be no more than a two- or three-day wonder before life returned to normal. He could handle that, but when repeat offenders threatened to disrupt the harmony at the club, that was another matter. Hence the common perception that as Smith pursued domestic and European honours from 1994–7, scarcely a week passed without some lurid misadventure cropping up in the papers, to delight the club's detractors. Ally McCoist has responded to the allegation that Rangers' philosophy could be summed up as: 'The team that drinks together wins together' with the logical riposte: 'If we had drunk as much as some people had made out, we would all have needed to book into the Betty Ford Clinic.' Some scurrilous rumours were spread by mischief-making Celtic supporters, and these were of such a libellous nature that even at this stage they dare not be repeated. But all the same, Smith certainly didn't have his problems to seek from the moment that Duncan Ferguson walked into Ibrox.

It might be harsh to describe the big striker as a ticking time-bomb, but more than a few eyebrows were raised when Smith confirmed that he had recruited the 22-year-old Dundee United player for a whopping £3.75m, not least because he had an aerial expert in his squad in Mark Hateley. Yet Ferguson's arrival seemed apposite in what turned into a surreal season for Rangers, in which 11 first-team players required surgery at various times and in which Smith was occasionally left striving to convince opponents that he had not sent out a bunch of fans by mistake. On the disciplinary front the manager's views were fairly ortho-dox: he asked for respect and courtesy, and for well-paid profes-sionals to behave as if football was their vocation. If anyone swaggered around acting as if he was a law unto himself, felt inclined to criticise Smith's selections publicly, or worst of all appeared to be picking and choosing which matches in which to offer 100 per cent, he would step in with a final warning, and woe betide the transgressor. 'It's a tough job, and you can't afford to be sentimental,' was his attitude. 'At the end of the day the club matters more than any individual, so you can't let star players do things which others in the team are forbidden from doing. That creates disharmony, and I won't have that. As soon as the players have walked into the dressing room, they are all equals in my eyes.' Smith meant it. Andy Goram had been one of the most luminous personalities in securing the treble, but when he started amassing excess weight towards the end of the outstanding season, and initially did not seem to notice that an issue was building up, Smith stepped in and placed him on the transfer list. To some observers beyond Ibrox this was regarded as a piece of shock therapy, but the manager was adamant and held a lengthy discussion with the goalkeeper during which he delivered his opinion that a hefty Goram could not possibly perform to his familiar, lofty standards. Goram, rather shame-facedly, pointed out that part of his training routine had been curtailed by injury, but he recognised that was no excuse, and when he returned for pre-season he was more than a stone lighter, and he subsequently shed additional poundage in preparing for a gruelling schedule.

Smith's man-management skills had reaped dividends again, but when Rangers were drawn against Levski Sofia in the opening round of the European Champions Cup – another new title – we were offered the first signs that the incessant struggle to master such European forays might be gnawing away at his confidence. Smith's options were limited by injuries to Goram, Gough, John Brown and McCoist for the first leg at Ibrox on 15 September but general incredulity was the reaction when Duncan Ferguson was included in the same line-up as Hateley, and asked to play wide on the left wing. Nor did the presence of Ally Maxwell, Gary Stevens and David Robertson at the back inspire huge confidence, even if this was widely assumed to be a fixture in which the Scots would canter to victory. For much of the home tie that view appeared justified, with Dave McPherson and Hateley sending their team into a 2-0 lead within 55 minutes. Whether they considered that the job had been completed or simply underestimated their opponents, they slackened their grip and the Bulgarians roared back into contention. Their two goals were a consequence of cringe-inducing gaffes from Maxwell and Ferguson, which were seized upon by Daniel Borimirov and the gifted Nikolai Todorov in the last 15 minutes. Even with the addition of a second headed goal from Hateley, a 3-2 score provoked jitters: it was as if Rangers could continually discover new methods of applying the self-destruct button. When they ventured to the intimidating arena of the Stadion Vasilij Levski, they started well enough during a deluge and seemed to be taking the sting out of the hosts' threat, only for Gough to make a hash of a clearance attempt and to hit the ball directly to Sofia captain Nasko Sirakov, who opened the scoring in the 36th minute. So far so inauspicious for the Ibrox men, but when it appeared that they would enter the half-time break in arrears, Durrant ghosted in at the far post and latched on to a Gary Stevens cross for the equaliser. That should have been the cue for a more aggressive approach, but having ripped Levski apart once, Rangers retreated into their shells, and they drifted further and further back as the match progressed . . . almost as if they feared that ignominy might be lying in wait. Dave McPherson probably should have steadied his team's nerves when he was allowed a free header from a Trevor Steven free-kick, but his powerful effort was within range of the home goalkeeper Nikola Nikolov, who produced a stunning save. The Bulgarians could not have anticipated that their winner would arrive in such dramatic circumstances. The travelling band of followers had endured the gamut of emotions throughout the 90 minutes, and suddenly their heads were in their hands as Rangers lost possession, Levski launched a breakneck assault and Todorov's ferocious shot from all of 30 yards was too much for the flailing Maxwell as it crashed into the net.

It was a wonderful strike from a gifted individual, but the angry shakes of the head among Rangers fans told the story, and recriminations arose over Smith's tactics and team selection: such questions were raised virtually for the first time in his managerial reign. Why had he chosen Duncan Ferguson and fielded him out of position? Why wasn't Alexei Mikhailichenko, a footballer who would have been perfectly suited for stemming the Levski menace, included in either match? Why was he persisting with Ally Maxwell in goals? Worse still from Smith's perspective was the perception that this most methodical of men had not carried out his research on the Bulgarians properly, and had paid a heavy price in failure to reach the Champions League group stages, which was to become a recurring theme as the decade advanced. Smith responded by stating his faith in the men he had picked – he could scarcely have done otherwise – but expressed disappointment at the fact that his club, who had gone ten games unbeaten in the previous season's tournament, had actually lost ground in the UEFA seedings. This baffled and angered him, and these issues festered in his mind throughout his attempts to pilot Rangers to European success. What could not be denied in the defeat to Levski Sofia was the fact that the Scots had initiated their own downfall, for three of the four goals they conceded sprang from the sort of basic errors that professionals should not commit.

An equally difficult start was noted on the home front as the club pursued their sixth consecutive league title. Several Scottish rivals showing signs that they no longer feared being thrashed by Rangers, and despite a 2-1 triumph over Hearts on the opening day of the campaign, their form was dreadful in the main. A number of performances left Smith seething during a spell in which they attained a solitary win in eight matches as a combination of injury accentuated by the absence of the hugely-influential McCoist, inconsistency and dearth of inspiration conspired to provoke an angst-ridden August/September. Smith worked harder than ever to pilot his team beyond the turbulence, as Craig Brown confirms:.

'Walter is one of those guys who doesn't blame others when problems arise. He knows that it is impossible to enjoy success all the time, so when things go wrong it only stiffens his resolve. Even the best managers go through rough passages where there is some negative flak from the fans and the media, but if you react to that or allow the criticism to affect your judgment, it usually backfires on you. Basically you have to say to yourself: "My methods were successful last year and the year before that, so I have to stick to my principles." And, if you do that, as Walter did, the good times will return again.'

By the start of October indications were that the mini-crisis was abating. Rangers secured an important 3-1 victory at Tannadice, then boosted their morale substantially by beating Celtic in the semi-finals of the League Cup at Ibrox. The result itself, a tight 1-0 win with Hateley making the vital breakthrough, came as a terrific fillip for all connected with the club, but it was the manner of the success which provided most of the reasons to be cheerful. Rangers were rediscovering the spirit of solidarity and tireless commitment, and that allowed them to transcend the red-carding of Pieter Huistra and still dominate their Old Firm rivals. By that stage too the redoubtable McCoist had recovered from his leg fracture, and he had played two full games for the first team and another substituting as Rangers prepared to meet Hibernian at Celtic Park in the League Cup final on 24 October 1993. As if to stress the impact that Smith had brought to Ibrox, he had in his sights a sixth successive domestic cup, and he had a dual motivation for wanting to maintain his sequence since Hibs had been the last club to beat Rangers in these competitions, eliminating them from this tournament at the semi-final stage in 1991. Ian Durrant sent his team in front only to see his effort swiftly negated by an own-goal from Dave McPherson, and with the contest finely balanced Smith cast a gaze at his substitutes' bench, and espied the glint in McCoist's eyes. With 20 minutes remaining it was time to play his trump card. Smith did admit that he was unsure whether the striker would be able to make a serious contribution, considering how little football he had experienced in recent months, but he need not have worried. Suddenly McCoist surged towards a loose ball with proceedings still locked at 1-1 after more than 80 minutes, and he sent the Ibrox fans into hysterical cheers when he scored with a spectacular overhead kick. 'Only Ally could have done that – and I told him that after the game,' said Smith, emphasising the bond which the men shared. 'It was a gamble to have him involved at all, but he can sniff out goals better than anyone.' But then McCoist had been Europe's leading goal-scorer in two consecutive seasons, and had gained the cherished Golden Boot for his prodigious exploits. To those who reckon that he was nothing beyond a high-class poacher, studying a video of that cup final will confirm that a master was at work, and that conjured out of nothing, his pivotal effort was blessed with a magical quality. One only has to scan the incredulous expressions of the Hibs players nearest to McCoist to understand why Smith valued him so highly.

Despite the surge of relief which enveloped Rangers in the wake of that cup victory, season 1993–4 continued to suffer from glitches. On the field the team were bolstered by the arrival in November of the effervescent Gordon Durie, who was an astute £1.2m signing from Tottenham Hotspur, but it would be straining credibility to suggest that the team achieved anything beyond grinding out wins. Nor did the ceaseless stream of injured warriors help to bolster morale, and in facing the press on Fridays Smith seemed to spend more time in medical mode than talking about football. Gough joined the sick list, followed by Durrant, and as New Year approached the manager went into the Old Firm clash at Celtic Park with his club filling the unfamiliar role of underdogs. Rangers stormed into battle though, given Smith's ability to lift his troops for these contests, and barely had the match kicked off before Hateley had pounced for the opening goal, after 58 seconds. It triggered a tremendous tussle, and the visitors were as resilient in this game as they had been prosaic in much of their Premier League challenge. Celtic, whose very future was being debated in the press and in the hostelries of Glasgow and elsewhere, were eventually overcome by 4-2. Watching from the technical area, Smith quietly nodded his approval of that display, and as the season progressed and his men clung on to their crown with unquenchable desire, he refused to criticise them for failing to replicate the stylish performances evident during the season past. As has been stressed on many occasions, Smith was a devotee of the virtues of substance and hard graft. His players reacted to victory over Celtic by mounting an unbeaten sequence stretching to 17 matches between February and April, including seven successive victories, which all but clinched another championship. 'It wasn't pretty for much of the time, but it wasn't just about their footballing ability, but also the physical and emotional reserves they had left to draw on,' Smith reflected. 'There was no time for them to relax or sit back and say: "Haven't we done well?" Instead it was on to the next game, the next competition, the next challenge. Week in, week out. And I couldn't have asked them for any more.'

❖

The boss, however, could have expected better from Duncan Ferguson, whose arrival at Ibrox had become shrouded in controversy. From the outset the youngster had looked ill-at-ease coping with the burden of expectations, and he repeatedly failed to convince the sceptics in serving up a series of indifferent displays which, coupled with his persistent injury problems and volatile temperament, marked him out as a liability. Worse still, having demonstrated an alarming penchant for turning any minor incident into a major stramash, the player found himself in the dock after head-butting Raith Rovers' John McStay. Given that this was not his first or even a second assault conviction, he had no grounds for complaint when he was sentenced to three months in Barlinnie jail, though his incarceration lasted only 44 days. Few among the Rangers' support regarded him as anything other than an expensive luxury, a 'ned with cash' as *Scotland on Sunday* described him succinctly. Smith though had some sympathy for his player, and he maintained contact with him during his imprisonment and even after Ferguson had departed Ibrox, as if to highlight his understanding of the pressures that surround those asked to dwell in the Old Firm goldfish bowl. Not that he was condoning the player's actions, but he recognised that when any young person is festooned with money and publicity, there is always the possibility of him going off the rails in a splurge of negative headlines. Especially if, like Ferguson, self-control did not come naturally.

Comprehending the dynamics of human frailty allowed Smith to contribute adroitly to establishing a sense of harmony in his dressing room. He knew it was impossible for 20 individuals to live comfortably in each other's pockets, and he accepted that rows, recriminations and even occasional violence would break out on the training pitch.

Some players required constant reassurance, others could communicate only by using the F-word, a few preferred their own company away from football, and others were desperate to become involved in as many late evenings as possible at Victoria's nightclub . . . without worrying whether the paparazzi ambushed them at the climax of proceedings. Smith appreciated these diverse attitudes without drawing the kind of ethical judgments which cropped up constantly in the tabloid papers. It was, and is, ironic that journalists, who are often less than moral exemplars, can heap opprobrium on young footballers for drinking to excess and enjoying other sins of the flesh. But while Smith's team selections or tactics might be the subject of criticism on occasion, most of his players revered him almost as a surrogate father. He could be grumpy and might scream at them, but he defended them to the hilt, and talked up their abilities whenever explaining was required in public. In return they invariably offered their utmost, and the consequence was a collection of trophies, a sixth successive league title, and a glut of media interest in everything relating to Rangers.

Perhaps it was appropriate, considering the troubled nature of much of the campaign, that the championship was sealed on an evening when the Ibrox side slipped to defeat, losing 1-0 to Hibernian at Easter Road. Though they finished the season much as they had commenced it, managing just two points from their final five fixtures, Rangers had done just enough to fend off their rivals. A weary, muscle-bound bunch of combatants journeyed home from Edinburgh that evening without enjoying a lap of honour after the final whistle, though the news that Motherwell had also lost in the twilight of 4 May ensured that six-in-a-row festivities could begin with a vengeance in Glasgow. According to one player, the gaffer proceeded up the aisle of the coach and thanked each of his men for the yeoman service put in during the season: 'Walter isn't a person for extravagant shows of emotion, but he was very grateful for what we had done, and I think that was probably one of the first occasions where it started to sink in that we were two-thirds of the way towards winning nine straight titles, and even though we were tired, there was this buzz about what might happen in the future. We had been warned not to raise the subject in any interviews, and Walter rightly thought we would be making a rod for our own backs if we made a big deal about chasing nine in a row, but let's not kid ourselves, it was high on our list of priorities. We had been ribbed about endlessly by Celtic fans from the days when we were growing up, so why shouldn't we talk about chasing their record, and if at all possible, beating it? And there was a feeling throughout the team that if we could win the league in '93–94 when nearly everything that could go wrong did go wrong, we could win it every season.'

Life was poised to change dramatically, at least for the other half of the Old Firm. In March, for a few hours at least, the unthinkable had almost happened when the Bank of Scotland threatened to send Celtic into receivership, before an outsider came to the rescue by acting as guarantor for the club's £7.5m debts. Some of us at the time believed that sum to be a drop in the ocean, but it was an indication of the sorry fashion in which the club had been managed while ruled over by the patriarchal Kelly and White families. It was Fergus McCann, a Canadian-based Scot, who marked the end of the fiefdom that had owned Celtic for the previous century, and set about remedying the malaise that had blighted the club since the mid-1980s. He had flown 'home' to Glasgow on 4 March and the following Monday he arrived as the new full-time chief executive and started to extricate Celtic from a financial mire, using expertise gained as an entrepreneur who had spotted an opening in the golf tourism market in Montreal, and transformed the business into a multi-million-pound operation. Some green-clad fans who were unfamiliar with stock-market procedures were initially unimpressed with McCann: to them he was a wee chap in a bunnet with a curious transatlantic accent. But there was no questioning his integrity, or his bank balance. 'I can now tell the fans that the club is safe,' he announced almost immediately. 'We have been able to resolve the critical short-term financing at Celtic, and shortly will be able to discuss long-term packaging.' If this sounded like the language of business rather than football, McCann was not fazed. He had a five-year plan for his new project, and claimed that he would not stay beyond that period. He wanted to inject the necessary funds to rid Celtic Park of the old Jungle and replace it with a gleaming, state-of-the-art stadium which would be the pride of Europe. And – music to the ears of the battle-fatigued supporters – he would release sufficient funds for the purchase of quality signings, who would terminate Rangers' hegemony.

David Murray viewed these developments from Ibrox with the studied indifference of one who would believe McCann's promises when they came to fruition, but not before. Walter Smith had never harboured the delusion that Celtic's slump would prove permanent, and in one respect welcomed the prospect of renewed hostilities, rather than being accused of profiting from the misery of another club. He recognised the fact that tribal loyalty requires a neighbour to beat, and that rivalry cannot exist in isolation. Obviously, given his position, there was no equivocation from Smith. He could neither afford to concern himself with his rivals' situation, nor would he concede that Scottish football was the better for a powerful Rangers and Celtic, a statement which he acknowledged was arrogant nonsense, the more so because the Scotland teams that qualified for five successive World Cups between 1974 and '90 contained only handfuls of Old Firm representatives. As Smith declared in the summer of 1994, he had enough issues of his own to address. He had to search for new blood for his squad and needed to ensure that there was no repeat of the Levski Sofia fiasco, so he scoured Europe in pursuit of players who would bring added oomph and sparkle to his line-up, and he enjoyed some success. He persuaded the gifted Danish internationalist Brian Laudrup to join Rangers from Fiorentina for only £2.25m – Duncan Ferguson had cost £3.75m – and recruited central defender Basile Boli from Marseille for £2m, which was a less gratifying piece of business. While Laudrup would eventually be acclaimed as one of the great foreign signings, there was no quick fix when Rangers launched their bid for a place in the lucrative Champions League against unknown quantities sporting the colours of AEK Athens. This was a pairing which again exposed Smith's inability to orchestrate a modified game-plan from the no-frills approach which worked in Scotland, but which too often appeared predictable and pedestrian against technically superior European adversaries, and this remains one of the more depressing of the club's continental encounters. Ewan Aitken, a lifelong Rangers follower and a bluff character who has visited many European countries, considers it to have been one of his most dismal footballing experiences, as he explained to me:

'We were basically treated like criminals by the Greek police, and there was no escape from them. The match was played early in August [the 10th] and the temperature was over 40 degrees, which might make you think would make anybody too lethargic to cause trouble. But it was just constant aggro from the cops, from the Greek supporters, from airport staff from the moment we landed in Athens, and we couldn't wait to get the match over with and get the hell out of there. When we got to the ground, we were manhandled outside the stadium, pelted with missiles inside, and as for the Rangers performance that night, they were just shite. Andy [Goram] was the only guy to do himself justice, and he actually saved us from a real tanking with a pile of excellent saves in the first half.

'But it was him against the world, and you can't keep them out forever when that happens. We were only 1-0 behind at the interval, but it could easily have been four or five, and when the striker [Dimitris Saravakos] scored his second goal with about 20 minutes to go, most of us thought to ourselves that we weren't going to pull this back at Ibrox. I have a lot of amount of respect for Walter Smith, but he screwed up big style that night. The defence [Richard Gough, Steven Pressley and Gary Stevens] was all over the place, and we read later that they had never played together in that formation before. Well, that is just daft, isn't it? And you can't blame anybody else for that but the manager.'

Smith accepted the responsibility: 'I tried the wrong defensive tactics for the game, and in the first half they didn't work.' He refused to shoulder any blame, though, for not preparing for the match as thoroughly as he should have done, pointing out that he and Archie Knox had watched AEK in advance, and had reached the conclusion that they were superior to Levski Sofia. Smith also mounted the valid argument that the tie had arrived before the start of the Scottish league season, and that it left such contests more reminiscent of a lottery than a Champions League. The defeat was swiftly followed by a reverse against Celtic, and suddenly a section of the fans who had been rejoicing in the spring reverted to appalling barracking of Smith and David Murray. I attended that Old Firm match, and reported in *Scotland on Sunday* that one or two supporters disgraced themselves by calling their chairman 'a f***ing cripple' within earshot of the press and a security guard. Some revisionists have alleged that this incident did not happen. It did. I was there. Smith had discovered yet again how fickle the soccer public can be, and the strain started to show. When AEK came to Glasgow bolstered by a home-made cushion, they again proved to be better than their opponents. Nearly 45,000 spectators howled for a sliver of inspiration or sophistication from their team, but Rangers kept punting aimless high balls towards Hateley and Duncan Ferguson, a double act that died on the big stage. Murmurs of unrest filtered through the stadium long before the end, and the nose-rubbing exercise was completed when Toni Savevski scored after 70 minutes, the prelude to a chorus of boos resonating around Ibrox. It had been a harsh lesson for Smith and his players, who crept off at the end, and the manager's latent frustrations exploded next morning when he was interviewed once again by BBC football reporter Chick Young. The unfortunate exchange went like this:

Chick Young, standing in the tunnel at Ibrox: *Would you agree that [Basile] Boli and [Brian] Laudrup didn't play well last night?*

Walter Smith: *I'm not answering that.*

Young: *What I'm trying to say is that you've gone out and spent at the highest level. But is the standard of play in Europe higher again? And are you going to have to match the likes of AC Milan to pay these types of fees?*

Smith: *I'm not following your line of questioning.*

Young: *Well, you spent £5m Walter, in the summer on good players, but these players are seemingly not good enough at the highest level in Europe.*

Smith, looking increasingly angry: *I don't think you can say that. How can you say that? I mean, they've just come here, and you've got to give everybody a chance to settle in. Are you saying that Boli and Laudrup cannae play in Europe?*

Young: *No.*

Smith: *Boli's won a European Cup-winner's medal, for f***'s sake, you cannae say he's no good enough to be in Europe. That's stupid, isn't it? You cannae say that Boli and Laudrup cannae f***ing play. Laudrup played seven out of ten games for AC Milan last season, and Boli played in the team that won the European Cup, and the only reason he didn't play last year was because his club [Marseille] were banned. You cannae say they cannae f***ing play in Europe. For f***'s sake!*

Young, getting more rattled: *At the end of the day . . .*

Smith: *Have you been up all night working that out?*

Young: *No, no, I'm . . .*

Smith: *Those were your f***ing words to me. That they couldnae play in Europe.*

Young tries and fails to interject.

Smith, shouting down the tunnel: *Archie [Knox], come and listen
to this f***ing interview. He's coming out with worse shite than
ever.*

Knox walks past with a furious glance at Young: *I'd have him
out of here on his f***ing arse if it was up to me.*

Pause.

Smith: *Come on, you cannae be f***ing serious.*

Young: *All right, I'll do it again. The Rangers fans are demanding . . .*

Smith interrupts: *Your questions to the chairman [David
Murray] last week were f***ing shite as well. If we had a bad
night last night, then you are having a f***ing horrendous morning the now.*

Young, meekly: *You did have a bad night.*

Smith: *That's what I said to you.*

Young: *But would you agree that the two of them didn't play
well?*

Smith: *Haud on, haud on, haud on, that doesnae mean they
aren't good enough to play in Europe. Surely they have f***ing
proved on many occasions before that they are good enough. It's
just f***ing silly to be talking about this.*

Young: *Okay, I gather that you're not happy with that. Let's
start again. What I'm trying to get at is . . .*

Smith: *That'll go down well at the Christmas f***ing party,
won't it!*

Interview ends.

The edginess inherent in this salvo demonstrates that Smith
occasionally has a short fuse when dealing with what he considers

to be stupid questions, but there again it was not that clever of Young to suggest that a player such as Laudrup, a prodigiously talented individual, would not make the grade in Europe. However, if the fire which burned in Smith was doubted, his response to the AEK debacle was instructive. Within weeks of crashing out of the Champions League, the manager had revitalised his troops and had maintained his domination over Celtic, who were still in the process of adapting to Fergus McCann's arrival, with a 3-1 victory in the early stages of the 1994–5 league campaign. It proved the catalyst for another of the long stretches of supremacy which typified this Rangers' collective. The team went 14 games without defeat and gradually amassed an unassailable lead, but just as they were homing in on their seventh title, a deep sense of sadness enveloped Ibrox and the wider environs of Scottish football. Davie Cooper, one of the most talismanic characters to pull on the blue jersey, suffered a fatal brain haemorrhage on Thursday, 23 March while recording a coaching film for youngsters with Charlie Nicholas at Broadwood Stadium. He was 39, and Smith reacted as one who had regarded the player with unstinting affection and admiration throughout his outstanding career. At Hillhouse Parish Church in Hamilton on the following Monday, he spoke movingly and emotionally of Coop's talents, his eulogy a fitting testament to the man who was gone too early. 'God gave Davie Cooper a talent. He would not be disappointed with how it was used,' Smith declared to a funeral congregation including many leading figures of the national sport. His words were acknowledged because of a tacit admission by some in the throng that it had taken an untimely demise for them to appreciate his gifts fully, and to recognise the routine derring-do with which he had sustained Rangers when they were languishing in the doldrums. Smith did not make that mistake. He was enraptured by Cooper's skills, and subsequently made his feelings clear that this was a character with talent to burn, who had borne a heavy load during strife that had damaged Rangers in the first half of the 1980s. 'The pressure on him must have been enormous,' said Smith, 'but the arrival of players such as Souness and Butcher allowed Davie the freedom to play. It allowed him the setting he needed, and he responded wonderfully. You can discuss his many match-winning displays and go into the details, but all that really needs saying is that Davie was a magnificent footballer.'

The death cast a pall over the latter stages of Rangers' league season, but Smith told his men to go out and perform in the style that would have brought a smile to Cooper's countenance, and they obliged with a series of sublime showings, and Laudrup was at the forefront of everything positive. Aberdeen were edged out 3-2 in April, and eight days later the championship was settled when Rangers beat Hibernian 3-1 at Ibrox. Title No. 7 was achieved by a resounding 15 points from Motherwell, who had fought courageously to remain in touch, but had lacked the resources of their rivals. Celtic, even with the financial stability offered by McCann, were not in contention, and their supporters started to inquire about finance for serious investment . . . not merely in bricks and mortar, but in top-class players. They gained their wish eventually, but Smith and Murray were not about to relinquish their grip on the Premier League, confirming that intent during the summer of 1995 when Paul Gascoigne arrived at Ibrox from Lazio for £4.3m, and Oleg Salenko joined from Athletico Madrid, Stephen Wright from Aberdeen and Gordan Petric from Dundee United. Attracting the Geordie Gascoigne, despite the quirks and demons that lurked beneath his jolly exterior, proved that Rangers had not relinquished the capacity to draw big names. Though some suggested that he was a spent force and still leant on the reputation he earned at the 1990 World Cup, he confounded that perception within weeks of pledging his allegiance to 'Glasgow . . . er, Rangers', though not soon enough to prevent Smith from experiencing another painful series of lessons on his team's less-than-magical tour of Europe. At least there were no slip-ups in the preliminaries, the Scots defeating Anorthosis Famagusta of Cyprus with a patchy home display at Ibrox when Gordon Durie scored the only goal. A much-improved showing away from home confirmed a 1-0 aggregate victory, but Gascoigne looked sluggish in these ties, and conceded later that his confidence had been low and that he was not properly attuned to the intensity of these matches. But his vitality resurfaced as he forged bonds with McCoist, Hateley, Durrant and other team-mates, this to the detriment of the clubs vying to halt Rangers' lengthy winning streak in league fixtures.

In the Champions League the Scots were placed in a 'Group of Death' with Borussia Dortmund, Juventus and Steaua Bucharest. It would be pleasant to relate that they made a seamless transition from thrashing such as Kilmarnock and St Johnstone, but that was not the reality. The campaign commenced with a workman-like display in Bucharest, but as so often in close-run affairs, Rangers were sunk by a single strike, in this instance emanating from Daniel Prodan. His 20-yard volley with six minutes of the tie remaining screamed past Andy Goram, who otherwise had had relatively little to do in goals. The Scottish team served up a worthwhile showing when they entertained Dortmund, gaining a 2-2 draw courtesy of Richard Gough and Ian Ferguson. Yet it was a portent of their Champions League travails that Brian Laudrup limped off at the interval during the contest against the German side, and he remained crocked for the next dozen games. In his absence, Smith was forced to grapple with the knowledge that he needed at least one win from the double-header with mighty Juventus, who could field world-class talents in Gianlucci Vialli and Alessandro del Piero, and that all Rangers' leading players required to peak at the same time. With the exception of Goram, this failed to materialise, and as they trudged into the Stadio delle Alpi, the team seemed to be preparing for a siege. The sight of honest journeymen in the mould of Alex Cleland, David Robertson and Stephen Wright preparing to do battle with maestros of their profession induced queasy feelings for those who had travelled to Italy. These did not abate, for in the first quarter of an hour Juventus weaved silky patterns through the visiting defence to such effect that they led 3-0, Fabrizio Ravanelli scoring twice with one from Antonio Conte. Men against boys, Armani v Barras, call it what you will: there was no disputing the evidence that for all the millions that had been spent by Smith in pursuit of a squad that could challenge the best opponents on the Continent, this was a humiliation. Neither did it offer consolation that they escaped from their ordeal with 'only' a 4-1 loss, because the suspicion arose that the hosts slackened their grip after netting a fourth through Del Piero: by then Cleland had been sent off for launching a swipe at the Italian icon. At least the Rangers man did not have to worry about meeting the same opponents a fortnight later. The manager, as was now usual, faced criticism for his tactics, though it was difficult to envisage any formation negating Juventus considering the depth of talent throughout their ranks. Rangers were forced to call up Gary Bollan for the re-match, and expectations were predictably low for the Ibrox clash. Despite a crowd in excess of 42,000, the atmosphere was dull and became even more so as the home team suffered a 4-0 defeat, despite mustering a performance that was considerably improved. All their commitment and industry counted for naught without a threat up front, and this was another evening on which, after Del Piero's early strike, Rangers pressed forward heroically and consistently without demonstrating the sharpness necessary to ruffle the visitors. If it was exasperating for the supporters, it was doubly galling for Smith as Ravanelli scored from an offside position and Moreno Torricelli and Giancarlo Marocchi completed the big haul in added-time.

Having amassed just one point from their four fixtures, it was surprising that Rangers still had an outside chance of progressing in the tournament, but this would entail beating Steaua at home and Dortmund away, and not even the most sanguine Ibrox supporters could envisage that scenario. To their credit, they produced some excellent football in both matches, including a magnificent solo effort from Gascoigne against Bucharest, which was worthy of a Champions League final. The Englishman's

50-yard incision past a swathe of Romanian defenders evoked memories of Diego Maradona's foray at the 1986 World Cup, but Adrian Ilie's goal ensured that his side left Glasgow with a share of the spoils. That trend continued in Dortmund where Rangers, basking in the Scottish trait of being carefree now that they had been eliminated, created myriad opportunities during a resplendent display which ended at 2-2: Brian Laudrup and Gordon Durie found the net, and German stars Andreas Moller and Karl-Heinz Riedle responded in kind. A downbeat group of players walked off at the end, not least because Gascoigne had been red-carded for two pretty innocuous offences, the second when he was furious not to be awarded a penalty in what seemed a credible claim. That incident perhaps summed up Rangers' European misadventures that season, namely that when they were not conceding soft goals or squandering opportunities up front, they were falling foul of officialdom, with Gascoigne alternating between classy and crass. Gazza's every action, gesture and indiscretion seemed to be captured by a photographer, presenting his manager with the dilemma of how best to save him from himself without extinguishing his innate enthusiasm. He embraced Gascoigne with human kindness and with verbal volleys when he felt these were required, as the former player recalls:

'I used to get it in the neck from him, and so did other players – but it was mainly me on the receiving end of his abuse. I seriously f***ed up one Friday night before a game, and he sent me away for three days. I was banned from Ibrox and told not to come near training. I was devastated by this, and never f***ed up again on a Friday. He also grabbed me by the neck on several occasions, and put the fear of death into me. I used to shit myself when he spoke to me – and that was when he was giving me praise.

'Yet I respected him immensely. I rate him right up there beside Terry Venables, and there are also touches of Sir Alex Ferguson in him. And the bottom line is that: I played for Walter Smith and Archie Knox. These guys were tremendous for me, they gave me my life back, and I will be forever grateful. With them, you had to be performing at 110 per cent, winning at half-time and full-time, and if you weren't, you were getting bollocked, because they were winners, pure and simple. There were times where I had scored one and set one up, and at half-time Walter would say: "You're just messing about, Gascoigne." And I shook my head, and he threw a boot at me.'

The other side to that dressing-room volatility was embodied in Smith inviting a lonely Gascoigne to Christmas dinner, after receiving a poignant phone call at his family home early in the morning. Within a few hours he and wife Ethel and their sons Neil and Stevie were sitting down to turkey with Gazza for company; I have a lingering notion that Mrs Smith might have been suprised, but reacted calmly, saying: 'Nuts, Paul?', 'Crackers, Paul?' until Gascoigne eventually asked his boss why he was being insulted. If one vignette epitomises why Smith forged a lasting relationship with one of the most troubled figures to perform for Rangers, his generous offer of hospitality was it. Ian Ridley wrote in *The Observer* newspaper: 'He had always been one of those people, like Sir Alex Ferguson who, when he first met the boy, saw something vulnerable in him that provoked a desire to take care of him. As Richard Burton's sister once said: "Rich had the kind of face that was too easy to forgive." '

A more pragmatic explanation for his benevolence was recognition that Gazza could act as an enormous asset to Rangers if his temperament and talent could be moulded to the task in hand. As 1996 unfolded the Rangers men were involved in a bare-knuckle scrap with a revitalised Celtic, who were as desperate as their supporters to prevent their Old Firm rivals from equalling or, heaven forbid, surpassing the fabled nine-in-a-row achievement. Fergus McCann was fulfilling his promise of bringing stability behind the scenes as well as delivering a magnificent revamp of Celtic Park, and just as Graeme Souness had done for Rangers under David Holmes, the club had recruited a series of high-profile signings. Dutch international striker Pierre van Hooijdonk had joined in 1995, to be followed by Jorge Cadete and Paolo Di Canio, a triumvirate who were swiftly branded the 'Three Amigos' by fans. As Celtic pursued their first title of the 1990s, where they had been porous, unconvincing and unable to mount a protracted challenge to Rangers, they were bursting with vim and vigour, and from Smith's perspective reflected a worrying sense of momentum. It was a measure of their transformation that they lost only one game in the league all season, at home to Rangers. The other Old Firm derbies were drawn, but pulsating spectacles in any case, the best being an engrossing clash at Ibrox which finished 3-3.

Smith required his elite players to carry the battle back to the opposition in such circumstances, and they responded. Hibernian were caught in the crossfire and demolished by 7-0, and Raith were briefly allowed to entertain thoughts of an improbable victory before a late McCoist double earned his side a 3-2 success. The pressure was on Gascoigne to help to spearhead a revival when Rangers, in one of their crunch matches, fell behind 1-0 to Aberdeen in Glasgow. Cometh the hour, cometh the footballer who would be the recipient of Scotland's Player of the Year award shortly afterwards and began to stamp his authority all over the visitors, bewitching and bewildering them to the delight of the home supporters. So what if there were occasions when it seemed that even he was not sure where his forays might take him? As McCoist remarked: 'If that was the case, what hope was there for the Aberdeen defenders who were trying to stop him?' Gascoigne scored two beautifully-worked goals which came with his trade-mark, and as the stadium was transformed into an inferno of tribal emotions, he coolly strode up to take a penalty and completed a hat-trick to cap what had been a personal triumph, a privilege to behold. That was instrumental in bringing Rangers their eighth title in succession, but the championship had proved to be a trek, not a sprint, and when it had been settled by a four-point margin, the club had to reflect on the fact they had lost two games more than Celtic, and would surely be confronted with even more fired-up adversaries in the season ahead. Smith remained objective: 'You can't get ahead of your-self in these situations. When you have won two or three championship titles, nine seems an awfully long way off in the distance. Then when you have six or seven, you feel that it might be coming within touching distance. But ultimately, getting this close just makes you appreciate what a great feat it was by Celtic in the first place.'

CHAPTER ELEVEN

NINE, NINE, NINE

❖

'If you don't win the league this season,
the other eight don't mean a thing'

As Rangers viewed the prospect of an achievement which would mean their supporters could counter mocking references to 'Nine in a Row' from Celtic fans, there was still no sign that the Ibrox club had cracked the code to guaranteeing better fortunes on the European trail. On the contrary, whenever football followers start to discuss whether Walter Smith or David Murray was more responsible for the successes of the 1990s, and whether Rangers would have fared better on continental business had they been playing in a more competitive domestic league, the answers tend to reflect the prejudices of those concerned, rather than answering why the light blues swept all before them at home, yet were constantly exposed on the bigger stage, give or take a few auspicious occasions. So far as the first question is concerned, it is undeniable that Murray's money was a massive factor in the metamorphosis from paltry crowds and an empty trophy cabinet in the early 1980s to the successful club that amassed silverware with ruthless efficiency a decade later. As numerous managers have proved when presented with wads of cash, and failed to transform it into tangible succes, there are few sure things in sport, and what counts in this debate are the opinions of the two men who led the Rangers' push towards nine consecutive championships. The mutual respect between them shines like a beacon. Walter Smith said in the mid-1990s:

'Basically in the modern game it is not managers who turn clubs into bigger clubs – chairmen do that. You need the right kind of driving force in the boardroom, and we have that in David Murray. He has never yet backed out of a deal. When we have needed players, then he has always found the money, and I just don't think that Rangers would be sitting in the position they are now without David. He is a hands-on chairman, and with the money which he has ploughed into the club, that's only right. But he won't stand still for an instant. He is an inspirational person, and it is a privilege to work with him towards a common goal.'

Murray reciprocated with a glowing tribute to the man that he promoted to the manager's role after the abrupt departure of Graeme Souness:

'Walter is the last of a breed, and I don't think that we will have another manager with his degree of integrity and loyalty. The Bosman influence on football is changing attitudes among managers as well as players, and no other manager will stay with one club for long periods. What we have to recognise is that Walter is one of the greatest managers Rangers have ever had.'

Thus the two men appreciated qualities in the other, which meant that though they had different areas of expertise, they were of similar opinion when it came to the weighty task of resuscitating Rangers and propelling them upwards. This is not to say that the club would not have thrived in Scotland had Souness remained in charge, though many have reservations on that score. What, for instance, would the fiery former Liverpool star have made of the chance to sign Paul Gascoigne? Would the obdurate Souness have relented in selecting McCoist, or allowed the striker to drift elsewhere, which would have been a horrrible example of man-mismanagement? How would he have coped with the chronic injury-list which bedevilled Rangers in 1994? One suspects that Souness would not have borne this burden as well as Smith, who implemented a superb patch-up job on his squad at regular intervals, and despite signing some players such as Basile Boli, Duncan Ferguson and Peter van Vossen, who at best flattered to deceive, could also point to successes such as Brian Laudrup, Gordon Durie and Paul Gascoigne, if one sticks to considering Gazza's contributions on the pitch. The puzzle over why Smith's Rangers struggled so badly in Europe is less easily resolved for those who recall how close his team came to beating Marseille towards the start of his tenure. By 1996 the majority of his players were well versed in the strictures of the Champions League; they acknowledged that it demanded a more patient and pragmatic approach from the helter-skelter of the Scottish professional game; and considering that Smith had enhanced his squad with Laudrup, Gascoigne and others, there genuinely was no excuse for the meek, tactically-naïve performances which were too often served up by Rangers.

Still, after being drawn against the Russian champions Alania Vladikavkaz in the qualifying round of the competition, it appeared that the Scots were poised to bring their A-game to the table when, having picked up a 3-1 advantage at home with goals from Derek McInnes, Gordan Petric and McCoist, they travelled to what seemed like the end of the earth – particularly for supporters who spent five days in transit from Glasgow to Vladikavkaz, via Copenhagen, Stockholm and Moscow – and produced an out-of-this-world display in annihilating much-vaunted opponents 7-2. It was one of those nights when McCoist buzzed in and out of the action like a cantankerous wasp, driving his rivals to distraction with a goal in just 33 seconds, and moving on to a hat-trick. Laudrup twice appeared on the score-sheet beside Van Vossen and Charlie Miller, and reverberations from the 10-3 aggregate were heard around the Continent. Could this be the season when everything fell neatly into place for Smith and his players? At first glance UEFA seemed to have handed Rangers a group, containing Auxerre, Grasshoppers of Zurich and Ajax, from which they had a definite opportunity to progress. However, any notions that securing the domestic title might be accompanied by a glorious march into the latter stages of the Champions League were dashed by a series of displays which varied from lacklustre to mediocre.

In preparing for the opening visit to Switzerland, which should have been targeted as a potential away win, Smith picked what on paper looked a formidable side, packed with flair and attacking threat from Gascoigne, Laudrup, Jorg Albertz, McCoist and Durie, but they produced what many Rangers' supporters believe was one of their club's worst performances on the European circuit in going down to a 3-0 defeat. Smith was furious by the climax, beseeching his men to remember the qualities that they had produced in eliminating Vladikavkaz; but there was no cohesion, a dearth of inventiveness and worst of all from the fans' perspective, a distinct lack of urgency within the visitors. They could, just about, tolerate their favourites being outclassed by AC Milan or Juventus, but certainly not by the unsophisticated efforts of the Swiss team. That reverse prompted derision at home from the non-Rangers' fraternity, and Grasshoppers' manager Christian Gross, soon to move to Tottenham Hotspur, dismissed his vanquished opponents with the words: 'They came here as holidaymakers.' Many Rangers' fans detected a semblance of truth in the comment, and Robert McElroy, faithful chronicler of all things Ibrox, was uncharacteristically apoplectic, summing up the evening with these comments:

'The Swiss could scarcely believe their luck. Rangers were lamentable, their appalling defensive errors typifying a pathetic opening to the campaign, and leaving many people to seriously question the tactical awareness of the coaching staff. Rangers, just possibly favourites to win the group given their results against the Russians, were rightly criticised, and scathingly so, and from then on were always struggling to maintain any kind of impact.'

For the next match, a home date with Auxerre, Smith predictably made several changes, but the introduction of Derek McInnes and Van Vossen did not fill the compact and competent French side with trepidation. Despite a better showing, which was certainly not difficult, Rangers slipped to a 2-1 defeat, Thomas Deniaud twice beating Goram and rendering Gascoigne's goal academic. Several aspects were now growing wearily familiar. Rangers had amassed 10 goals in disposing of Vladikavkaz, but had scored once in 180 minutes against two distinctly average sides. That toothlessness was evident too often season after season, and McCoist's limitations had grown painfully obvious during European excursions, especially when he found himself pitted against defenders who could back-track quickly. In the midfield industrious toilers in the shape of Ian Ferguson and Derek McInnes, who could guarantee satisfactory shifts for Smith on Saturday assignments in the Premier League, were devoid of the vision and class to chart a path through their rivals, and for all that Goram and Gough were usuallly excellent, they frequently found themselves surrounded by colleagues who were out of their depth.

It was scant comfort for the manager. Off the pitch, the long-term failure of Rangers to invest in an academy structure, the norm across Europe, had often appeared to be a major mistake, and there was a limit to how much more investment Murray could pour into the Ibrox coffers. Hence the anti-climactic nature of the exit from the Champions League, with Rangers trounced 4-1 by Ajax in Amsterdam and edged out 1-0 in the return match, before finally mustering something for their fans to cheer about with a 2-1 success over Grasshoppers, sealed by a McCoist double. But the sorry saga concluded with a 2-1 defeat at the hands of Auxerre. Mitigating circumstances could be put forward in one or two of these matches: Rangers were missing a dozen players for their second tussle with Ajax, and their first joist with the Dutch club was disfigured by the adolescent behaviour of Gascoigne who, with no regard for his colleagues, aimed a petulant kick at Winston Bogarde, and was immediately dispatched from the field as an incredulous group of Rangers followers looked on.

At least for the beleaguered players and coaching staff, the quest for the Premier League title offered a smokescreen in the aftermath of what had developed into a thoroughly dispiriting continental venture, and the fans who had jeered with derision at the shambles in Zurich and Amsterdam were soon roaring approval as Rangers moved into the one setting which mattered more than any piffling European fixture: an Old Firm derby. Ibrox was packed to its 51,000 capacity when Smith's team entertained Celtic on Saturday, 28 September – three days earlier, when Auxerre had shown up at the stadium, the attendance was 37,344, the smallest of the season. 'Nothing could beat these occasions for the supporters, and especially with all the talk about us going for the ninth title,' said Richard Gough. 'One of the fans came up to me at the start of the season and told me: "You know, if you don't win the league this year, the other eight don't mean a thing." So, no pressure there then.' But as Gough and his team-mates recognised, this was a pivotal period for the traditionalists, men who had grown up routinely employing the F-word any time that they mentioned Celtic, and woe betide Smith's players if they did not keep to their part of the bargain. Smith observed mildly: 'It's not like in other countries where teams are allowed the occasional slip without having half the city screaming at them. Here Celtic and ourselves have to win every single week, or we don't hear the end of it. It means that we are constantly forced to attack and go forward, and when we come up against a side like Auxerre, who don't have the same pressures, they have the defensive edge over us.'

It was a valid observation, but as the manager well knew, words counted for little in the build-up. Hence the buzz around Ibrox as the hosts strove to shrug aside their Champions League disappointments, and attend to the sharp end of business.

Rangers were purposeful and penetrative from the outset, and despite the labours of an evolving Celtic team the afternoon belonged to the men in blue, their 2-0 win the consequence of goals from skipper Gough, described by Smith as his 'cornerstone', and Gascoigne, whose season flitted from joyous high to dismal low, and back again. It was indicative of the inconsistency of Rangers during that momentous season that their Celtic success was the precursor to a five-match sequence in which they managed only one victory. Then it was time for another Old Firm slug-fest, and an opportunity for Celtic to lay down a marker that they believed they could halt Rangers' title aspirations. Sadly for the Hoops, once again their strikers were posted AWOL in a scrappy, nerve-shredding affair at Parkhead, which appeared set for stalemate until Laudrup conjured up a mesmerising goal with a thundering effort from 25 yards. It was another reminder of the powers of this individual, as creative as he was carefree. Smith beamed at the media after the match, and confirmed: 'That is one of the things which makes Brian special. He can change the whole course of a match in a few seconds.' It was an apt summation to describe the Austrian-born Dane, whose exploits with his brother Michael had illuminated the 1992 European Championship, when they celebrated their country's unexpected triumph. Though sceptics might wonder why Laudrup, an individual of unquestionable European pedigree, did not hit the heights on a more regular basis in the Champions League, his talent was sufficient to induce approval from most objective Celtic stalwarts.

Rangers had established a 100 per cent record over their Old Firm opponents at the midway point of the campaign, and Smith's success against the principal rivals was, and is, a remarkable feature of Scottish football. I talked to a number of former players asking how he psyched up his teams for these high-octane occasions, and was half expecting to be told that the manager delivered a blood-curdling speech, full of copious references to 1690 and 1916 and 1972, but their response was surprising. One player said:

'Walter knew that we knew the history behind the Old Firm; he knew that we knew the songs and the religious baggage which goes with the territory; but what he didn't have control over was discovering how we would react to the massive pressure which comes with these games, and that was why he would sit us down and chat about it on the Fridays before the match. It wasn't all fire and brimstone, although Archie [Knox] would get us all fired up the closer we got to the kick-off. Walter's method was to tell us quietly, man to man, that Rangers was a club with proud traditions, and that he expected us to go out and perform as previous generations of players had done, for the club, for the supporters, for the honour of being able to play when there were thousands of supporters inside the ground who would have bitten off their right arm to have the same opportunity. And he told us that he wanted all of us to be able to look at ourselves in the mirror at the end, whatever the outcome, and know we had done our very best. Of course he was aware that even the most talented and toughest of individuals can crack in the Old Firm environment, so he tried to make us all feel part of a continuing story, and when I look back it was very, very effective strategy. Because anybody who might have been inclined to get tied up in knots in the countdown to the derby was constantly being reminded that they were part of a big family. And, as we always told each other, families look after each other, whatever is happening.'

That comradeship was one of the admirable facets of Rangers' charge, but controversy was never far away from several players, whether in Goram seeming to lend his endorsement to the UVF on several occasions, or Gascoigne's car-crash existence threatening to spiral out of control in an orgy of excess. There was also a growing campaign by Scotland's other clubs against what they perceived to be the pro-Ibrox bias of many officials operating within the Premier League structure, and that thorny issue reared its head for the third Old Firm meeting, in January 1997. Smith's team had accumulated a near-impregnable lead in the championship, and their rivals arrived at Ibrox knowing that only a victory would suffice, but they were rocked by a stunning Jorg Albertz free-kick. Despite clawing back into contention, they fell 2-1 behind in the 83rd minute when Erik Bo Andersen capitalised on a defensive lapse. Undaunted, the visitors roared back on to the attack, and suddenly Portuguese striker Jorge Cadete latched on to a header deep inside the Rangers' penalty area, and whipped the ball into the net for what would have been a deserved equaliser on the balance of play. But the celebrations were stalled when the stand-side linesman flagged for offside, and Rangers fans bellowed approval. Andersen added his second, and the hosts had one hand on the championship trophy once more. The controversy sprang from the fact that this did not constitute an everyday cock-up by an official. Television pictures proved emphatically that Cadete had been comfortably onside when he had collected the ball, and that he had not strayed offside when he had polished off his shot. Even to the naked eye it looked an awful call, and yet Scotland's two main tabloid newspapers hardly mentioned the incident the following morning. What they did eventually reveal was that the linesman at the centre of the dispute was a Rangers season-ticket holder, who drank in his local masonic club and was a self-confessed 'loyal' fan of the Ibrox organisation. None of which should have come as any great surprise, and yet it sparked a new surge of paranoia among Celtic supporters, some of whom hired a private detective to investigate the origins and backgrounds of those that they suspected of being too favourable to Smith's club.

I remember watching an interview with Walter Smith during that period. He was calmly discussing what it would mean for his players to collect the championship title, and standing next to me a normally quietly-spoken colleague of the Celtic persuasion became increasingly agitated until he could stand Smith's satisfied countenance no longer. 'Ach, awa and f*** yourself,' he shouted at the screen. 'Do you know why your team is so crap in Europe? It's because there are no masons over there to give all the decisions in your favour!' In three sentences this usually rational fellow encapsulated the hysteria that pervades the Old Firm milieu, explaining why the internet is a receptacle for barking-mad conspiracy theories. It's all in there lurking in blue and green cyberspace: rumours of SFA collusion in Celtic punishments, so-called coincidences, whereby a well-known referee will be spotted adjacent to an Old Firm player, rants against political correctness by those who see nothing amiss in wanting to be up to their knees in Fenian blood. And so on. Mercifully, the likes of Smith and Tommy Burns have been able to rise above the ordure which emanates from both sides in forging warm friendships, but anyone who still doubted that Scotland had a distance to travel before it could be regarded as a grown-up country should have been around the hostelries of Glasgow and Lanarkshire in March 1997, when Rangers completed a clean sweep of victories over Celtic with a scrappy, unmemorable 1-0 win, the deadlock broken by Ian Durrant, whose lob reached the net after a mix-up in the Celtic goalmouth. In anyone's language it was a rotten spectacle, but as the victors readied themselves for their celebrations, many Celtic supporters booked holidays specifically so that they could avoid being in their homeland when the ninth league championship in a row was secured.

Rangers' boss kept his counsel and attempted, vainly, to quell some of the triumphalism that had swept over the massed Ibrox ranks. On Wednesday, 7 May a date forever ingrained in the minds of thousands of Rangers acolytes, the team ventured to Tannadice, where a win would seal the championship. His side had been beaten 1-0 there earlier in the season by Dundee United, but in this instance nothing was about to ruin the festivities, and when Laudrup seized the clinching goal with a header, it was the prelude to a spree of gargantuan proportions. It was the early hours of the morning before the players arrived back at Ibrox, but the streets around the ground were jam-packed with thousands of celebrating fans, for whom the prospects of work next day, or the Friday even, would be as remote as the rings of Saturn. They howled for Smith and McCoist, Gough and Laudrup, and gradually the scale of what had been achieved sank in. Smith's principal emotion was to thank his lucky stars that it was all over: 'The feeling at the end of the game was relief. Knowing how much it meant to Rangers' supporters, it is something that we will never forget.' Nearby Richard Gough was awash with joy and exhilaration:

> 'I was very emotional. Even my wife commented on it. She said: "I saw you on the TV, and you had tears in your eyes when you received the trophy. You never even cried when I had the kids." But we just had to keep going until we did it. I was injured with about six games to go, but we were playing Celtic, so I said to Walter: "I'll play, because if we beat them, then we'll have won the league." And we won. But then we lost the next three matches, and we had to win one out of our last two games, so we almost took it down to the wire. I can't speak highly enough about the guys and about Walter and Archie and the chairman, and this is one of the greatest moments of my life. And, you know, the boys are legends now.'

That they were, and if critics attempted to raise the European issue, Smith and his charges could afford to shrug off the jibes, not least because no British club in the Champions League in the early 1990s at least came as close to marching to the final as Rangers. My belief is that Smith moulded a side in his image: unprepossessing, wholehearted, occasionally dour and defensive-minded, but prone to flashes of inspiration and panache. Perhaps his Rangers teams would have thrived if they had been allowed to enter some form of British league at their zenith, for no other reason than Smith, akin to Sir Alex Ferguson, understood perfectly the dynamics of the game as it was contested in the UK, where physicality and pace held sway over any aesthetic sensibilities. If it was his and his team's misfortune that their style did not adapt well to Europe, Smith could counter with the retort that Rangers were at least masters on their own patch. For tens of thousands of Ibrox fans who toasted their ninth title, that was quite enough.

CHAPTER TWELVE

Exit Strategy

❖

'Nerves jangled to the accompaniment of
obsessive media coverage'

By the summer of 1997, Walter Smith was exhausted. His methodical approach to management meant that when he was not preparing for important matches, he was studying videos, checking on opponents, fulfilling behind-the-scenes functions which are the lot of any football boss, and committing himself to the intensive media scrutiny which demands a constant approach to fire-fighting and news management. He had been at Ibrox for more than a decade, and as manager he had copped the flak for six years and more, and as he neared his 50th birthday even this most passionate of football adherents was in urgent need of a break from the game. The players noticed it as did David Murray, who was also aware that there was no question of preventing Smith from fronting the Rangers campaigns for another season, particularly the pursuit of an unprecedented 10th consecutive championship. As the season started early on 23 July when the club were involved in a Champions League qualifying tie against the Faroese minnows FC Gotu, a sense of unease hung around Ibrox, exacerbated by the dearth of time afforded the manager as he strove to assemble virtually half a new team in the space of a few weeks.

Possibly recognising that it was no longer sufficient to persist with a largely-Scottish side bolstered by a few guest artists, Smith had signed an Italian quartet made up of Lorenzo Amoruso from Fiorentina, Sergio Porrini from Juventus and Perugian pair Marco Negri and Rino Gattuso, in addition to recruiting Swedish midfielder Jonas Thern, whose previous career had been spent in the main at Napoli and Roma. On the face of it, several of these individuals boasted obvious qualities, and the acquisition of Gattuso, who was considered one of the brightest youngsters in his homeland, hinted at a long-term policy for adapting to the rigours of the Champions League. There is little purpose, though, in spending millions of pounds on new players – the above cost £14m in total – if they are not permitted time to integrate into the existing structure and to find their feet in a new country, whose football philosophy is radically different from the domain of Serie A. Sad to relate, if this was Smith's last throw of the dice, it yielded a pretty dismal return.

European missions had begun to morph into Smith's version of the film *Groundhog Day*. He could change the names on the jerseys and tinker with tactics, but he seemed unable to alter the outcomes. No-one was surprised when Rangers cracked a bundle of goals past ineffectual FC Gotu for an aggregate of 11-0, with McCoist and Durie contributing three goals apiece. While they were able to luxuriate in the role of dominating small fry, it was also no surprise that the team would encounter problems when pitted against Swedish club IFK Goteburg in the second qualifying round. The contrast between the performance of Rangers' strikers when they met second-rate adversaries as opposed to those who belonged in Europe's top tier was conspicuous. Events at the Stadion Ullevi followed the well-worn path for supporters who had kept faith only to behold another demoralising collapse by Rangers, after they had seemed to weather the storm in progressing to half-time without their goals looking especially under threat. Any delusions of adequacy were quashed upon the resumption when the Scandinavian side scored twice in two minutes through Stefan Pettersson and

Par Karlsson. It might have been supposed that Rangers would seek out a precious away goal, but they retreated into their shells apparently unsure whether to strive for containment or to risk being expansive. In the absence of clear guidance from the technical area, the visitors succeeded in conceding a third goal, finished by substitute Peter Eriksson. One could criticise Smith for the second-half slump, and a section of supporters did begin to raise misgivings over what they perceived to be the manager's inflexibility and persistent tactical blundering. This was justified in the circumstances, and the trickle of complaints quickly intensified when Rangers bowed out of the Champions League after drawing 1-1 in the second leg. The tide of frustration turned into a deluge after the club's short-lived sojourn in the UEFA Cup, in which French club Strasbourg, who were struggling in their domestic league, beat the Scottish representatives by 2-1 in both matches, the first of which was notable for Brian Laudrup visibly appealing to Smith to alter his approach. As the jeers increased from the brassed-off support and the media rounded on the management, it must have seemed a long, long time from May to September for those in charge, but if change was required, it would not be rushed.

Murray had resolved that he would not be railroaded by the tabloids or by any interests into implementing precipitate moves, yet the financial implications of his club's latest European fiasco could hardly be ignored. He recognised that Smith was unwell and suffering from the strain of such stalwart service, so the two discussed the situation at the beginning of October, and decided on a compromise. Smith would stay in the job until the end of the 1997–8 season, and his exit would be confirmed at Rangers' annual general meeting later that month. It was not an ideal arrangement, but it confirmed two things: that Murray, despite his reputation as a hard-nosed businessman, could be impelled by motives which, if not sentimental, had less to do with the stock market than ensuring that his long-term ally was not dispatched with indecent haste, and that Smith was not interested in hanging around unless he felt that he could continue to drive Rangers forward. He offered initially to stand down immediately, but that proposal was peremptorily rejected by the chairman. When the agreement was announced on 28 October Smith received a standing ovation from shareholders before he had had an opportunity to speak. He explained, as he struggled to hold back tears, why he considered it best to pave the way for a successor:

'There were pressures on the players which led to difficulties in the European scene. That to me has been a disappointment. However, I felt that a lot of the pressure came from me as the manager and that, after Strasbourg, I was beginning to become a problem with the players. There was a growing sense of anti-climax about the job. Rangers were not given any credit for beating Hearts in the Coca-Cola Cup last year. I went to the press room after the game, and it was like a morgue. There was no sense of achievement. It was: "Oh, they've won it again, now let's get on with it." There was a realisation on my part that things were changing for me. The next day's papers all focused on complaints that a foul had been committed on the halfway line in the build-up to our fourth goal. That had an effect on me. I didn't get any feeling of a great sense of achievement. But I decided to carry on because of Nine in a Row, and what it meant to everybody.

'The expectations of the club became greater with every championship we won, and obviously that led to more pressures. There have been times when I have been through periods of severe criticism in the press. A lot of demands are made on you. There are lots of pressures, but it's the same for the players. In Europe last year [v Auxerre, Grasshoppers and Ajax] I felt that we could have done far better than we did, and I felt there was a lot of pressure placed on the players because of the pressure on me. After the Strasbourg defeat, there was a cry for the manager to leave, and I felt that me being manager was going to create a problem for the playing staff. There is no divine right for any club to be successful, but I do feel that in the next few years we will have the opportunity to play and compete at the highest European level more than we have had so far.

'A new coach will need support. We need to be slightly more tolerant than we have been, and I hope everybody will look at the club in a new light. The fact is that a new coach could lose out early in Europe, and nobody will blame him, and quite rightly in my opinion. We need patience, but I have every confidence that we will succeed.'

The jumble of thoughts was not typical of Walter Smith, but it revealed the conflicting emotions beating in his breast. Denunciation from Rangers' fans had clearly riled him, though he could live with or without the media's views, but he recognised his complicity in the unacceptable string of European results. What may have irked him most was the tacit assumption that any manager could have enjoyed similar success in his position, which was manifestly untrue. When asked later about whether he was aggrieved that his achievements at Rangers had been unfairly overlooked, his reply was illuminating. 'I probably do when I look back on it, but my personality has a bit to do with that. I don't actively seek headlines, and I like to keep myself to myself. But, still . . . 13 trophies in seven years . . . nobody else in modern times has done it, and I am proud of that. Generally, things went pretty well.' Smith was entitled to a spot of self-congratulation, but true to type preferred to leave the tributes to others, and these personalities could speak for themselves. Tommy Burns, the former Celtic manager, struck the right chord in commenting:

'The old cliché will apply, but it will be true. Namely, Rangers won't know what they had in Walter until he's away. In fact the Scottish game won't realise what it had either until he has gone. I do not have the slightest doubt that Walter would be a success if he moved to England. I sincerely hope that he has not grown too disillusioned with the game, because he has what it takes. He has shown that repeatedly, and while figures like Alex Ferguson are exceptional, Walter Smith could come down here and do something similar.

'The truth is that I have never had anything other than total respect for Walter. I always held him in the highest esteem, because he knew what managing a club of Rangers' size was all about. He always conducted himself with dignity, especially when he was living with the added pressure of trying for nine in a row. And I always felt comfortable and safe whenever I was in his company. That for me was a true measure of the man. Even though he won nine titles in a row, Walter still found himself under pressure if he lost a few games. That's very tough to deal with, but he has handled himself marvellously throughout the years. So no-one should ever undervalue what he has done, and even though he was able to spend a lot of money, there was much more to it than that.'

As for chairman Murray, his words reflected the relationship that he had established with Smith over a decade, but also indicated that whatever the desires of the fans, he was not obsessed with amassing records for records' sake. His priority lay in making the correct appointment, and if that meant missing out on a tenth championship, he was sanguine about the prospect:

'I will work closely with Walter to find the right manager. We are looking at someone who will be northern European and certainly English speaking, and it would be beneficial if the new manager could settle in during the last couple of months of Walter's reign. We aim to be properly focused and move towards a future, which I am convinced will be bright. There will be changes because we have to move with the times, and these changes mean there will be no more bouts of indiscipline at the club. I couldn't believe the standing ovation Walter got at the AGM. I have never heard anything like it. It was very emotional, and I have to admit that I had a tear in my eye. Walter feels he needs a change in his life, and we respect that entirely. He is one of the greatest managers Rangers have ever had.'

The words about indiscipline point to Murray's exasperation at the fashion in which Rangers players were as likely to feature on the front pages of Scotland's newspapers as in the sports sections. There was a spat in a kebab shop involving Ian Durrant and Derek Ferguson, which also involved the constabulary; Andy Goram blundered into murky sectarian waters when he agreed to switch on the Christmas lights in Belfast's Shankill Road, and subsequently sparked fury by allegedly wearing a black armband in honour of the UVF terrorist Billy Wright; as for Paul Gascoigne, whose marriage to Sheryl had ended with sensational stories involving wife-beating and drunkenness, the disintegrating player was caught mimicking playing the flute, a ubiquitous instrument in Orange walks, in front of Celtic's supporters. There were few depths left to plummet. It might seem strange that all this, and more, transpired under Smith's stewardship, but there again the manager was a disciplined figure in a rock-solid marriage, who stuck to his own limits when it came to socialising, and refused to be a nursemaid for adult players. This did not mean that he ignored responsibilities, but acknowledges that Smith had a hundred chores to attend to on a day-to-day basis, and he could not be expected to issue curfews to his stars, particularly when so many of them were injured for sustained periods between 1995 and '97. The fact that most of his leading personalities, including Goram, McCoist, Hateley and Gascoigne, were sidelined for months at a time allowed them to be out of sight, if not of mind, and it is a dangerous situation when young men consumed with self-pity seek refuge in alcohol and decide to pour out their hearts to the nearest football groupie.

❖

In the aftermath of Smith's declaration at the annual meeting it appeared that he would be offered another post at Ibrox, and for a few days at least the club was a haven of sweetness and light. Having thanked his players for their efforts prior to delivering a paean to Murray, Smith paid homage to his back-room staff in terms which explain why, wherever he has ventured, Archie Knox has rarely been far behind: 'The boys in the coaching room have been fantastic, and it hurts me a bit when they are criticised for their efforts, as none of them could possibly have given any more. Archie could have been an outstanding manager in his own right and has loved being here, while the rest of the staff have been wonderful, and have contributed greatly to our success.' It was patently the end of an era, and Smith emphasised how much he was moved by the spontaneous applause that he had received at the AGM:

> 'Of all the things that have happened to me during my time here, that ovation before I spoke was probably the best of them all. It was totally unexpected. As a manager you often feel alone in the middle of it all, and it is easy for people to criticise what you are doing. But without a doubt that ovation was the best thing that has ever happened to me, and it was very difficult to start talking afterwards. I couldn't believe what the shareholders did, and I will always be grateful to them.'

The search for his replacement commenced with the media speculating on the appointment of, say, Kenny Dalglish, Bobby Robson, George Graham or Terry Venables, disregarding Murray's insistence that he was looking to Europe for Smith's successor. As the hype intensified, many so-called exclusives amounted to nothing more than a journalist phoning a name and asking if he was interested in the job; if the answer was anything but a blanket refusal, the story would be turned on its head and appear under a headline similar to 'Rangers Swoop for X'. Eventually tiring of some of the more ludicrous suggestions,

David Murray agreed to conduct an interview with BBC Scotland, telling viewers:

'Walter has had far too much to do. It was unrealistic, and the guy badly needs a break. What's more, the days of the football manager as we have come to know it, doing everything, are gone. We are looking for a coach as opposed to a manager. There is a football side to the job and a business side to the job, so we will do exactly that. The coach's job is a massive job in itself.

'I have read with interest several newspaper stories linking the likes of Dalglish, Graham and Robson with the Rangers job. Now that gets these names out of the way, and we can get on with things. Basically we need a top-class first-team coach, some-one who has a proven track record in Europe, someone who has done it. But you can rest assured that we will have the new coach well in place by the end of the season to give him and Walter as long as possible together before the new coach takes over com-pletely.

'Walter will be very much involved in the process of finding the new coach, and there is no doubt that we need continuity with the coaching. Walter was recently away for a couple of days looking for players, and that meant two days where he was away from his own players and the coaching. We can't have that. We want the coach to identify the players he wants, and then it will be up to a chief executive or myself to take the negotiations forward.'

Most of these discussions seemed to assume that Smith would carry on in some capacity at Ibrox, yet those who watched Smith and Knox for the remainder of the season had no doubts that they would not be outstaying their welcome. One such evening at the old and dilapidated Brockville Park was witnessed by a Falkirk supporter, Robbie Strang, and he related his memories of how the Smith regime sputtered towards its close. 'It wasn't a good night. The rain was pouring down, and the wind was howling, so you wouldn't have anticipated Smith and Knox being in the best of moods. But their shoulders were slumped, they both looked absolutely knackered, and the expression on their faces screamed the message: "We would rather be anywhere else than here!" It was pretty clear that some of their older players were either reaching the end of the road [Durrant, McCoist] or were on the verge of being moved on elsewhere [Goram, Gascoigne] and although their fans chanted "Nine in a Row" every so often, even the majority of them seemed to appreciate that it wasn't going to be ten titles, given the upheaval around Rangers at that stage. My own belief is that the team had shot its bolt, and perhaps the axe should have been wielded a bit sooner by David Murray, because once you have announced that somebody is leaving a job but is not actually exiting for the best part of seven months, he is dead in the water.' Such a verdict might be considered slightly harsh, considering the manner in which the Premier League race developed into a white-knuckle ride before the outcome was resolved at the start of May. As for the Old Firm derbies, Richard Gough's goal settled the first meeting and Marco Negri secured a draw for his team at Celtic Park. Something rather arthritic was noted about Rangers' display on 2 January and Laudrup was correct to observe that Celtic 'were just hungrier than us today' as his side slumped to a 2-0 reverse. And yet there was nothing between the clubs when they met again in the final league fixture of the season at Ibrox on 12 April.

The force was with Smith's line-up on the day. They had eliminated Celtic from the Scottish Cup the previous weekend, and they had recorded five consecutive victories as they prepared for battle, a pattern that was maintained in a furious struggle. The visitors enjoyed most of the territorial advantage in the opening quarter, but could not break through; then Jonas Thern produced a magnificent 30-yard strike which flashed past Jonathan Gould in the Celtic goals. Smith's men held a vital advantage which they did not relinquish. This was vintage Rangers, a throwback to the days when they had toyed with opponents, and Jorg Albertz, who was at the centre of the action, sealed the spoils with a goal in the

66th minute. This left the Old Firm rivals locked on 66 points each with four games to go, but Rangers boasted a superior goal difference and were clearly on a roll. No. 10? Surely! That assumption might have been justified if Smith had been presented with the option of tackling Celtic over the course of these matches, but a minefield of awkward games had to be negotiated instead. Nerves jangled to the accompaniment of obsessive media coverage reflecting views from both sides of the great divide as if the issue was as important as the Middle East conflict, and the scope for mishaps grew. Celtic were first into the fray on the weekend of 18/19 April and beat Motherwell emphatically by 4-1, which meant that Rangers had to travel to one of their bogey grounds, Pittodrie, to eke out a win. In a contest which demanded discipline and precision, the Glasgow club missed several fine chances and paid the price as Aberdeen edged home by the only goal, which handed the initiative back to Celtic. The following week Rangers weighed in by trouncing Hearts 3-0 at Tynecastle, which added fuel to the fire of conspiracy theorists who claimed that the Edinburgh side would lie down to Rangers when required; Celtic could only draw 0-0 against Hibernian. Pulsating stuff. On 2 May, as pressure on both teams reached absurd proportions, Rangers hosted Kilmarnock and their striking profligacy again let them down as the well-organised and efficient visitors silenced the stadium by orchestrating a 1-0 success, which even with news of Celtic's 1-1 draw with Dunfermline dealt a severe blow to hopes for Ten in a Row. The scenario was now straightforward: Rangers had to win their final match away to Dundee United, and hope that Celtic would come unstuck at home against St Johnstone. Smith was on the verge of departing Ibrox and knew that he would be remembered as a Rangers hero whatever occurred on 9 May, but nagging away was the question: is there room in the script for one more shock? Celtic soon made sure that their own script would go according to plan with a 2-0 triumph that rendered Rangers' 2-1 success irrelevant. So near, but blue-garbed fans reflected that matches which their team had strolled through in previous seasons had now become difficult exercises, and where once the likes of McCoist could taunt opponents, now it was as though he was running into a stiff breeze. Hence the need for a new Rangers coach.

One last date remained on Smith's calendar, 16 May, which brought the opportunity to mark his farewell from Ibrox by winning the Scottish Cup final against Heart of Midlothian. Two years previously, Brian Laudrup had been in devastating form as Smith's side thrashed the Edinburgh club, and it was predictable that Rangers were overflowing with sentiment along the lines of 'We'll do it for Wattie' as they headed to Celtic Park, though the departing manager would take nothing for granted. Hearts were awarded a contentious penalty by referee Willie Young, which was calmly converted by Colin Cameron . . . with fewer than 90 seconds on the clock. Thereafter came a series of vignettes rather than a full-scale performance from Rangers. McCoist at 35 was still capable of precipitating panic within opposition ranks, but the parts did not add up to a convincing whole, and the Ibrox men seemed down and out when Stephane Adam scored for Hearts early in the second half. Rangers launched a sustained offensive, as if recalling their lines from memory, and Gilles Rousset was forced into a couple of excellent saves before McCoist struck with seven minutes remaining. It was a cracking contest, but it finished as it had begun with thousands of Rangers fans screaming derision and disgust at Young after McCoist was denied what seemed a certain penalty, the official decreeing that he had been pulled down outside the penalty area. Laudrup's ensuing free-kick drifted wide, and despite a lengthy stretch of extra-time, Jim Jefferies' team hung on for a victory which was well merited over the piece.

Smith was dignified in the aftermath and congratulated Hearts on their success, praising the improvements that they had made in the previous two seasons. As he soaked up what he must have envisaged would be a last hurrah from the Ibrox support, he refused to hang around and gatecrash the winners' parade. It was not the result that he had desired, nor had the season unfolded as planned, but no individual in football who achieves 13 trophies in seven years can be adjudged to be a failure. Though weary of fighting the good fight, Smith had only recently turned 50, and other battles would ensue and other disappointments would need to be endured. For the moment, though, he could afford a wry smile of semi-satisfaction, for was that not the cry 'Walter, Walter' ringing out from the blue-and-white ranks encamped around the stadium? Not bad for a Rangers man who had stood amid the throng 40 years earlier.

CHAPTER THIRTEEN

Bad Times at Goodison

❖

'The voices of doom were in full cry on the Mersey'

After he left Rangers, Walter Smith was able to relax on holiday and to spend time with his family and to catch up with Iron Maiden, Bon Jovi and other choice selections from his rock collection. But considering his exploits in Scottish football and the high esteem in which he was held by Alex Ferguson, Kenny Dalglish and other prestigious names in the English Premiership, it could only be a matter of time before he was persuaded to dip his toe into the water in England. Would he go to the right place, a setting in which he would be allowed appropriate amounts of money and time to forge the camaraderie which had been one of his priceless assets at Ibrox? Critics who believed that his success had been due to David Murray's financial clout would not be slow to pounce if he walked into a high-profile post south of the Border and fell flat on his face. Any job offer can look attractive, though, if it happens to include false promises. Everton was where he chose to pledge his future, despite the fact that the Goodison Park club had been routinely lacklustre for a long time. The Liverpool club were not the first prospective employers to contact him, for Sheffield Wednesday had made an initial approach; but Smith was tempted away from entertaining Hillsborough's offer by promises made to him by the Everton chairman, hamper tycoon Peter Johnson, which were never delivered. The problems stacked up almost from the outset, according to BBC football writer Phil McNulty:

'Johnson had said there would be massive transfer funds and unlimited ambition. Walter was given money to spend, and invested it wisely on the then unknown midfielder Olivier Dacourt, and the Scotland and Monaco star John Collins. But Smith was then stunned to discover that his brave new world was being financed by money which Everton didn't actually have. The banks were banging on the door, the club were facing a financial crisis, and Smith was shown the signpost towards future mediocrity when terrace idol Duncan Ferguson was sold to Newcastle United behind his back by a desperate Johnson, who needed to raise quick cash. Goodison folklore even has it that Smith's wife Ethel knew about the Ferguson deal before her husband did, because he was otherwise engaged preparing for a game. Smith was tempted to quit, but it was Johnson who left and opened the door for [theatre impresario] Bill Kenwright to fulfil his dream of owning Everton, and the new chairman immediately handed Smith an extended contract – but some people called it a longer sentence.'

It did not require much study by Smith to realise that he was in a precarious position almost from the off. What should not be forgotten is that he had arrived at a club who had only narrowly avoided relegation under Howard Kendall, because their goal difference was superior to that of Bolton Wanderers, and prompted by Johnson any manager might have been captivated at the prospect of launching a renaissance for the other Mersey-side organisation. Yet so much of what Smith had to deal with involved cost-cutting, entrenchment, seeking bargain-basement buys and resorting to purchasing senior players who were well beyond their prime. He assessed the situation from a clinical perspective, in hindsight:

'My time in the Premiership helped me as an international manager, because it showed the necessity of stability. We had 86 transfers in three-and-a-half years at Goodison. I never had a team which was mine. I signed [Marco] Materazzi and [Olivier] Dacourt when they were young. I signed [Thomas] Gravesen. But when Peter Johnson put the club up for sale, the bank said we had to start selling players. So I began my second season with 38-year-old and 39-year-old centre-halves Dave Watson and Richard Gough. If anybody thinks that was through choice . . . and it wasn't their choice either. I have to be honest when I look back and say that I made a number of errors, but . . . signing David Ginola, Paul Gascoigne, that wasn't the way that I wanted it. I was fire-fighting. And I'm sorry that was the case, because it's a great club with a fantastic following.'

Despite the friendship which blossomed between Smith and Kenwright, money was in short supply, and the Premiership was not meant to support charity cases, especially as Manchester United, Arsenal and Liverpool were threatening to pull away from the rest of the opposition. Yet one feels that Smith, with the knowledge that he had accrued from his spell at Dundee United, should have been rather more adept in the transfer market, particularly given his renewed links with Archie Knox. I ventured down to the club to speak to the two men on a Thursday in the winter of 1999, and they were courteous, good humoured and clearly relishing the chance to avoid the suit-and-tie appearance which was demanded at Ibrox. What was missing, though, was any sense that they were in the job for the long haul or that they genuinely believed they could drag Everton out of the bottom half of the division. Smith, probably realistically, had set his sights on the lowish side: 'The same rules always apply: you have to strive your utmost, even though your level of ambitions may be different at a club such as Everton. There wasn't going to be a situation where you would be aiming to beat Manchester United every week. But there was no reason why we couldn't accept the challenge to be as good as we could be.' A practical approach perhaps, but it was hardly designed to win over the supporters, and this helped to explain the antipathy which gradually increased between the Scot and a section of Everton's fan base, who saw him as dour, uncommunicative and set in his ways. By contrast, those followers who met the manager spoke of his warmth, sense of humour and restlessness at being unable to provide the punters with a squad that could mount a sustained championship challenge.

Alan Nixon wrote in *The Independent* newspaper:

'His desire for stability at Everton was ultimately undermined by his own lack of achievement. The manager who came south of the Border with silverware-strewn credentials from his time at Rangers took his time to sort out the squad he inherited, made some poor signings, fell out with too many players and was betrayed by some of the club's biggest earners. Duncan Ferguson's return was a catastrophe, Paul Gascoigne's high-profile capture a sad sham and the deal for David Ginola a badly-judged investment. When Bill Kenwright backed Smith with cash recently, he signed three midfield players when the side cried out for a striker. Smith is a genuinely nice man, perceived as dour for his interview style, but sociable away from football and with a dry sense of humour. Once, after I had written that he was considering quitting, we met in an Italian restaurant and rather than rant, he was warm and amusing. When asked how close the trattoria was to his home, he replied with a grin: "I just rent up the road. Of course, I won't be staying." '

And he did not lay down residential roots on Merseyside, as if indicating that his tenancy was destined to be brief.

It was surprising in some respects that he lasted as long as he did. Everton were humiliated 3-0 in the fourth round of the FA Cup at the end of January 2001, and a group of fans immediately called for his removal. Rumours of dissent in the dressing room were circulating as were allegations that he could not motivate some of his star performers, and Smith went on the counter-attack:

BAD TIMES AT GOODISON

'If the players were not trying hard enough and the lack of passion was a recurring theme, only one man is to blame, and that is the manager. If that's the case, he should be sacked. A lot of things have happened over the period where we have been dogged with an inconsistency, and that is something that has never been more prevalent than this season. We have had a huge turnover of staff and we have had constant chopping and changing in terms of team selection almost since I arrived here, so it has not been an easy situation for anybody. But listen, you have to remain optimistic in football, because if you can't be optimistic then you shouldn't be in the job. So while our battle to push the club into a good position is still ongoing, hopefully we can do that in the future.'

Smith kept tinkering with his formations and recruiting new personnel, the abiding impression being of a conveyor belt of itinerants passing through Goodison rather than a team being created gradually. By March of 2002 the voices of doom were in full cry on the Mersey, with justification, as their heroes had managed but one win in their past 13 league matches. The final straw came on 10 March when they were bundled out of the FA Cup 3-0 by Middlesbrough, almost without a whimper of defiance. Kenwright's face told the story – he recognised that the axe must fall, but he hated having to sharpen the blade. There was no alternative, and within 48 hours Smith had been sacked for the first time in his career, unemployed at the age of 54. 'I think after nearly four years working at Everton, there is bound to be a painful feeling on the morning after you learn you have to leave,' he reflected. 'I think every manager faces the possibility of being asked to leave, but you hope it doesn't happen to you. But it has happened, and I just have to face up to that." He pointedly refused to use the word sacked or dismissed, which hold dishonourable connotations for a person who had grown up in an industrial heartland. 'At this stage it is very difficult to say that I have enjoyed being here. There have been highs and lows, there have been lots of good things and a lot of things I have enjoyed during my time here. It hasn't been easy, but overall you feel a sense of frustration, coupled with a level of disappointment.' Kenwright's regret could hardly have been more evident: 'The difficulty here was the finality of ending a working relationship with someone who, on a level of integrity, stability and honesty, is as fine a human being as I have ever been associated with. We made the decision which we felt was right, and he took the news like the true man of honour that he is. In fact, Walter was absolutely extraordinary, because he ended up talking about trying to be helpful for the future of the club. It has been a privilege to work with him during the last three years.'

Smith's spell in the Premiership must be judged as a failure. He failed to pull Everton out of the bottom half of the division, and they were in danger of being relegated when he was replaced by the more youthful David Moyes, who responded with diligence and guided Everton to the safe haven of 15th place: the club grew stronger with each season thereafter. It sums up the essential decency of Smith that even his detractors could not accuse him of being anything other than honest and committed in his dealings with players, supporters and administrators. 'Perhaps I made a slight error in picking Everton, in that it was the right club, but not the right time,' he said. 'I wouldn't make that mistake again.' Where would he go next? His analytical skills made him a personable television pundit, but there was no great urgency to manage again if the circumstances were not right. At least until he heard the Tartan Army wailing in the style of the First World War recruitment slogan: 'Your Country Needs You'.

CHAPTER FOURTEEN

REVIVING THE THISTLE

❖

'Everybody is happy to join up with the Scotland squad now'

As Walter Smith's life moved into 2004, it resembled that of a resting leading actor with ample finances earning interest in the bank. He had been released from the irksome task of having to deal with agents and reporters on a regular basis, could spend as much time as he desired with his family, and attend to business at his Glasgow hostelry The Rosevale. He could fit in rounds of golf whenever it suited him and his coterie of former players and managerial contacts, and even develop an interest in gardening. But an individual such as Smith was never likely to be content with bowing out quietly from football, and if he did not actively seek employment, he kept his finger on the pulse. He watched aghast the decline of his country's team under Berti Vogts, and maintained lines of communication with senior figures in the game. It was with a slight sense of incredulity, however, that Smith received a telephone call one morning early in March from the Manchester United manager Sir Alex Ferguson, asking whether he would be interested in travelling to Old Trafford and working as his assistant for the remainder of the Premiership season. He would be filling the shoes of Carlos Queiroz, who had departed previously for Real Madrid. Smith declared that this was not the sort of invitation that any person in soccer refused, and though the invitation 'felt like something out of a movie', he had barely informed his wife before he was heading down to join his Glaswegian friend: 'The chance to come to Manchester United was something that I couldn't turn down. There are few bigger challenges in football than helping a successful side sustain their achievements. I have huge admiration for what Sir Alex has achieved at United, and I am excited to be a part of it.' He knew in advance that his stint would be a short one, and he recognised that Ferguson's team had suffered an unexpectedly difficult season, but that was immaterial. As the tracksuit was pulled on again in readiness for dealing with players of the calibre of Ruud van Nistelrooy, Ryan Giggs and Paul Scholes, he felt refreshed and back on the beat where he belonged, even if the scale of the Premiership club's resources took him aback:

'It was incredible, even after everything which I had been party to in the game. It wasn't just the 67,000 people at every home match and the worldwide fan base, where you received constant reminders of being way in excess of what is attached to any other club, but I also wasn't prepared for the demands placed on the players. Everyone wanted a piece of them. All the time. I knew what I was brought there to do, and I would like to think that I justified the faith shown in me by Sir Alex. In my opinion, to judge United on this season is to take their achievements out of context. In the past 11 years they have had a third-placed finish, but in winning eight titles in that time they have never failed to claim the championship in back-to-back seasons, and that is a marvellous record by anybody's standards. In fact before I came here I always considered that Sir Alex was one of the best managers the British game has produced. But now after seeing him at close quarters in a club environment, seeing how he pulls together the vast number of strands of the job, I know he is the best.'

After his brief spell at Old Trafford Smith's return to the footballing mainstream with the Scottish national side thrilled not only the man himself, but the frazzled onlookers who followed the team's relentless slide down the FIFA world rankings to the high 80s, which was below Burkina Faso and Syria. A cottage industry of grim humour was up and running (*If the Scots couldn't do well against Iceland, they could arrange fixtures with Tesco and Asda*) as a demoralised group of individuals found confidence draining away with every fiasco against the Faroes or mess-up in Moldova. Though Smith became an obvious candidate to replace the ineffectual Vogts, he was far too diplomatic and mindful of his own experiences to be seen actively touting for the post. His response to inquiries: 'Taking charge of your country would appeal to the majority of managers, but I don't think that it helps the man currently in the position to talk of replacements. I had to deal with this when I was at Everton and to a degree at Rangers, and I feel for others who find themselves in the same circumstances.' The clamour only heightened in the months ahead, and though some criticism of Vogts may have been excessive, with whiffs of xenophobia surrounding several columns written in his denunciation, it was absurd to hear a few Scottish players complain that there was a language problem with the German manager, considering that one or two of them could hardly string a couple of coherent sentences together. Vogts' deficiencies were self-evident: he lost the media, lost the Tartan Army and lost to most of the minnows in Europe, or so it appeared, and the outcome was inevitable as 2004 neared its end. Alternatives to Smith were limited, not least because he was available at short notice and seemed ideally equipped for the job of Scotland manager. The expected dismissal of Vogts and appointment of Smith, confirmed on 2 December were greeted with a mixture of delight and relief. Craig Brown commented:

'This is terrific for Scotland, and it will be applauded by the media, all the supporters and the players, who will realise they have got a great manager. His main quality is his coaching ability backed up by excellent man-management. I don't know a single player who says anything other than that Walter is outstanding, and he will definitely change things for the better and gain a positive response from the players.'

The view of the ex-national manager was echoed by former Scotland internationalist Gordon McQueen, who touched on one of the key attributes which Smith would instil in his men – the belief that while miracles happen rarely in sport, they were always possible in the febrile sphere of football:

'We have the most optimistic supporters in the world, but at this moment in time even the Tartan Army has lost confidence in the side. I think he has got to win the fans back and do things that Berti wasn't doing, and I have every confidence in his abilities, because he has seen it all before. The great thing about this job as well is that he will have the whole nation behind him.'

During the first weeks in charge, Smith sought to reinforce that impression by asking the former Celtic manager Tommy Burns to work with him, and persuading his old Ibrox comrade Ally McCoist to bring his enthusiasm and ebullience to the Scotland hierarchy. These appointments earned him popular acclaim, as did the positive front that he immediately displayed towards press and broadcast representatives, many of whom had felt ostracised by Vogts. 'Media-wise you need experience,' he said. 'We have a population of only five million in Scotland, yet we have more newsprint than England, more national dailies than England. So part of handling any situation in Scotland is handling the media, and Martin O'Neill did that brilliantly when he was at Celtic. Now when I took over, the Scotland players had been threatening a boycott of the media because of the level of criticism they had been getting. That isn't the way to go. And as an experienced manager, I was able to come in and point that out to them.' He also sought to engender good relations with the clubs by trimming the excessive number of friendly fixtures which had been orga- nised by Vogts. Friendlies were the bane of a club manager's life, according to Smith, and his methodology was clear. There would be a cessation of internationals organised simply to bring money into the SFA or Sky TV's coffers, and he would concentrate on establishing a scenario where every match was invested with significance. When Smith had stepped into the role, Scotland's prospects of qualifying for the 2006 World Cup were slight, but he was focusing on the wider picture, which meant that no player was ruled out of contention, and these included exponents who had retired prematurely in despair over the chaos which had permeated the previous regime. He quickly assembled his first squad, and delivered an honest assessment of his priorities to the players in the affluent surroundings of Mottram Hall in rural Cheshire, where he had linked up with Burns and McCoist. As usual there was no soft soap or flannel, but a lucid exposition of where everybody stood in his plans:

'I felt it was more important to get these lads together to outline the future than to play a match at this stage, because it is a matter of urgency that we reduce the number of call-offs the Scotland squad has been suffering over the years. We had our first talk last night, and I told these players that I thought they were the ones who should represent their country. But I also emphasised that they would all have to show willingness to come along whenever they are selected. It's a question of achieving a club mentality with an international squad, and you can't do that if players keep failing to turn up.

'Some aspects of the previous regime had to be adjusted. There were some poor results in friendly matches. This led to a poor spirit amongst the players, and the heavy criticism they took over their performances and results proved to be demotivating. So we need to address how many games we tackle. As things stand we are insisting that players join us when selected, but we have to create an environment where they are keen to be involved. It's part of the first step of the process, which is to regain a little respectability in terms of everybody's view of the national team.

Hopefully that will lead on to improved results, because my goal is exactly the same as that of any other international manager – to help steer the team to qualification for European Championships and World Cups.

'I know that it will not happen overnight. But equally we don't have time for boys. Whoever comes into the team will have to stand up and be counted straight away. Younger players have no time, in the same way that the manager has no time. It might be hard on them, because international football is a difficult arena in which to gain the necessary level of experience, but that's the situation we are in at the moment.'

Smith's debut game as manager came in March against Italy, who were heading towards being crowned kings of the world. It was a tough proposition in the forbidding setting of the San Siro in Milan, and considering the limitations in resources at his disposal. It is instructive to examine the footballers that he selected to confront the Italians. There was no sign of a Baxter or a John-stone, a Law or Dalglish: this was a functional group of hard-working individuals who were being asked to shoulder a nation's expectations. The line-up that started comprised Rab Douglas, Jackie McNamara, Steven Pressley, David Weir, Gary Naysmith, Gary Caldwell, Paul Hartley, Barry Ferguson, Nigel Quashie, Lee McCulloch and Kenny Miller. On the bench sat Craig Gordon, Neil McCann, Andy Webster, Brian O'Neil, Stevie Crawford, Garry O'Connor and Russell Anderson. Smith declared in ad-vance that the performance was more important than the result, and that he wanted his men to be disciplined and strong-minded and prepared to chase every single tackle for 90 minutes. It may not have sounded like an aesthetically-pleasing formula, but Smith had few options when pitted against opponents who were world class in most positions, and if the Scots had to resort to being honest artisans, so be it. The most-capped player in their ranks was David Weir, who was back after a 30-month absence, and at the other end of the spectrum the wide midfielders

McCulloch and Hartley had amassed four minutes of international experience between them. The visitors' aspirations may have extended no further than exorcising the spectre of recent drubbings – 5-0 versus France, 6-0 against the Netherlands – but the Scots at least performed with the gritty resilience which can be anticipated from teams under Smith's tutelage. They blocked their opponents and disrupted their attempts to ease into a silky passing game, their energy and industry beyond reproach. After AC Milan defender Andrea Pirlo had swept a resplendent free-kick past Douglas after 34 minutes, and the stricken goalkeeper had to leave the field, still Scotland scrapped and snapped at their rivals' heels. If the Tartan Army did not have many thrills served up in attack, the majority realised that this was a night for consolidation and composure, and they roared their approval on every occasion that McCulloch or Weir or another Scot stifled the threat of Totti, Gattuso or Pirlo.

Smith looked on with an appreciation of the qualities of the hosts – 'They will be up there with the best at the World Cup next year,' he noted presciently – and with obvious pride considering the robust display from Scotland, who showed tenacity in greater measure as the contest progressed without looking capable of redressing the balance in goals. There were occasional moments to savour with Quashie latching on to a Miller flick which forced the Italian goalkeeper Gianluigi Buffon to parry the ball narrowly past his post, and Miller being released by Barry Ferguson for a run through on Buffon, which should have asked more of the keeper: Miller was able only to muster a stabbed shot that was comfortably saved. These shafts of menace were encouraging, because Scotland's recent efforts at posing a striking threat in their Group 5 fixtures had been thoroughly unconvincing. As the game approached its climax, one or two hopeful Scottish supporters started to harbour hopes of a late goal and a memorable outcome, but it was the Italians who scored in the 84th minute when the peerless Pirlo profited from a rare Miller transgression with another masterly free-kick, which he drove past the diving

Craig Gordon. A 2-0 score probably better reflected the gulf between the combatants, but Smith's side had soaked up considerable pressure and handled the occasion well enough for the press to be fairly appreciative of their efforts. The verdict of *The Sunday Herald* was typical of the tone. 'Losing by just a couple of goals represented a precious return to some form of respectability,' wrote the estimable Michael Grant. 'Without getting too excited about what was no more than a stuffy, dogged performance, Scotland at least showed an ability to compete with clearly superior opponents, and this is a time to be grateful for small mercies.' Smith had never been under any illusions that this was a long-term project with a limited squad, and though talented youngsters were emerging from within the SPL, he would have to grow accustomed to perspiration rather than stardust.

A sprinkling of green shoots of recovery had been witnessed in Italy, and the consequence was a capacity crowd at Hampden Park for Smith's next match, a World Cup qualifier against Moldova at the beginning of June. This was a chance for the Scots to recompense fans for the dreadful display that they had served up when the sides had met towards the end of the previous year. Despite the reveries harboured by the Tartan Army that a renaissance was underway, Smith remained cautious and mindful of the dangers of meeting east European opponents and underestimating their abilities. Other managers might have reacted angrily to the words of the Moldovan coach Victor Pasulko, who ventured to suggest that the Scots were no better than his own side and had no outstanding talent, but Smith was canny enough to respond in measured tones:

'It is a realistic appraisal on his part. We drew over there, and in their home game with Norway they drew and we lost, so he has every right to say what he has said, but now we want to show him a different Scotland side, and prove him wrong. He's not out of order in his comments, but it is up to us to change his opinion. We have to take responsibility for giving the fans something to shout about, and I have said as much to the players. What I am looking for is consistently improving displays. If we get them, the results will follow, but we must achieve a good standard, especially when in possession of the ball. Moldova have set out their stall to be defensive even in home matches – that is the way they play; good luck to them – and the onus is on us to counter that tactic and impose ourselves on the game. But I am not expecting it to be easy.'

His suspicions were well-founded. Scotland were cheered on the turf as if they were conquering heroes, but were by no means convincing for much of the occasion, and their opponents belied their negative reputation with a series of fine attacking moves which, with the benefit of cooler heads, might have granted them the lead. There was even that unnerving sound of mass murmuring at Hampden, denoting the crowd's grumbling or fears, or both, over what they were watching. A blank score-sheet after 45 minutes was not what they had envisaged. Smith refused to flap, and the introduction of Christian Dailly and James McFadden eventually paid dividends as both scored goals. The visitors were eager opponents, constant thorns in the flesh and bones of the Scottish defence, so the 2-0 victory represented a minor success in the grand scheme of things, and Smith was quick to embrace Pasulko when play ceased, as if to tell him: 'You were right.' Given the horrors which had induced a deathly pallor among Scottish followers in 2003 and '04, any victory was to be savoured, and it helped to lift Scotland off the bottom rung of the group table. When they gained a no-scoring draw against Belarus in Minsk a few days later, the signs were definite of solidity returning to the ranks. A record of played 3, won 1, lost 1, drawn 1 was hardly the stuff of legends, but Smith was warming to his national task, and Burns and McCoist had slotted into their berths with the harmony which can prove so productive between Old Firm protagonists. Smith dealt out praise all round:

'The reaction from my players, every single one of them, has been fantastic, and while we have only got them for a short period of time before every match, we have worked hard to build up a good atmosphere, and there is definitely a buzz now. The back-room staff are a big part of that, and Tommy and Ally have been tremendous. I got Ally involved because I'd had him as a player, and I knew he was one of those lads with a personality that can lift any room and body of people, and he has done that.

'Everybody is happy to join up with the Scotland squad now, which was maybe not always the case in the last couple of years when there was a lot of despondency. Now we have a decent level of intensity on the training pitch, and more importantly we now have get-togethers where we talk, play golf and have a couple of drinks. It has worked very well, and we have moved forward. But clearly there is still a long way to go.'

❖

The Scottish mood had changed dramatically. Where once it had appeared that their team's World Cup dream would have to wait until the next qualifying campaign, a rising tide of confidence envisaged Scotland fighting back into contention despite a hazard-laden fixture schedule in the autumn, with trips to Norway and Slovenia and the return meeting with Italy. The Tartan Army tend to be a volatile unit, and in detecting renewed reserves of discipline and desire in the side's efforts under Smith, it was only a short step to imagining that they could start making tentative travel plans for Germany 2006 the following summer. Come September the Scots prepared to entertain the Italians in a match from which tangible reward was required if Smith's men hoped to prolong their involvement in qualification. The fans knew what to expect from the bold Walter and his players, and his sensible approach to making the best of his raw material simply added to the unity between the players and their acolytes. Marcello Lippi, the cerebral Italian coach, recognised that it would not be sensible for his compatriots to indulge in an overly-sophisticated game plan and plumped for the towering front pairing of Christian Vieri and Vicenzo Iaquinta with the imposing if ageing presence of Francesco Totti set behind the duo. Smith and Scotland were undaunted, and as *The Glaswegian* paper commented: 'These are the kind of days you dream about.' For long stretches of the game the Tartan Army were able to wallow in what-could-be after Kenny Miller scored with a 12th-minute header, which vamped up the atmosphere into a frenzy of nationalistic fervour. What made Miller's contribution all the more critical was the fact that he was the only fit first-choice striker available to Smith, which cast the Wolverhampton Wanderers player in a lone role in front of a four-man midfield of Barry Ferguson, Darren Fletcher, Paul Hartley and Nigel Quashie. Living on their nerves and wits, the Scots survived a barrage of pressure from the Italians, for whom Vieri squandered a golden opportunity in ballooning a short-range effort over the bar. It was a reprieve which allowed those watching to wonder whether the *Azzurri* might fail to breach the home defence, but cold reality returned in 76 minutes when substitute Fabio Grosso scrambled an equaliser after a corner from Mauro Camoranesi. It was no more than Lippi's team merited, considering the fashion in which they had constantly striven to be enterprising and attacking, but it was a 'scunner' in the local parlance. The match finished 1-1, which still gave the Scots something to play for against Norway, but the mission was near-impossible.

Which made the performance in Oslo four days later a triumphant vindication of the sense of purpose and unity that had spread through the ranks of Scotland's finest. The mission to the Ullevaal Stadium would constitute a pivotal test of Smith's leadership, for this was the type of fixture which his countrymen had lost the habit of winning. From the outset Scotland bristled with intent and served up a dominant first-half display, which was too hot for the Scandinavians. After 21 minutes James McFadden headed on a Ferguson cross, and Miller sent the ball past the stranded Thomas Myhre; after 30 minutes the prolific striker capitalised on Andre Bergdolmo's error and again lashed a shot past Myrhe. A third goal would have killed off Norwegian hopes, and Miller had the opportunity to collect his hat-trick as half-time approached, but his effort struck a defender and bounced to safety. Despite a rally from Norway in the second period after they had made three changes, the Scots were tenacious when they had to be. Craig Gordon pulled off a string of fine saves, and Neil McCann almost sealed matters in the 75th minute with a fine shot which this time was parried expertly by Myrhe. It was a superb performance despite Ole Martin Aarst's late goal, and Smith leapt in the air at the conclusion of the game. On taking the job he had stated that one of his key objectives was to make Scottish people proud of their national side again, and this showing provided stark proof that his team were on the rise. The manager had no control over results elsewhere, and Norway could derive comfort from the knowledge that if they beat Moldova and Belarus in their remaining ties, they would progress whatever the Scots did in their corresponding fixtures. Perhaps Vogts should have been sacked earlier by the SFA, with Smith granted the whole of the World Cup qualifiers to weave his magic.

Such speculation was rendered irrelevant when Belarus travelled to Glasgow in the first week of October. It was widely perceived that they would pose minimal problems at Hampden, but they emerged with a 1-0 success, courtesy of an early goal from Vitaly Kutuzov, and Scotland could not retrieve the situation. That confirmed their elimination from the final list of World Cup participants, and it created a miserable climax to an impressive second half to their campaign. But then the Scots ventured to the Petrol Arena Stadium in Celje to meet the Slovenians in their final group fixture, and reverted to the stunning form which had been evident in Oslo, winning 3-0 after Darren Fletcher, James McFadden and Paul Hartley had found the net. If ever a four-day period exemplified the contrary nature of Scotland's footballers and helped to explain why so many managers have walked away from Hampden Park engulfed in profound bafflement about the national psyche, this was it. But Smith could not afford to linger on the Belarus setback. As he glanced back on his first year in office the manager could embrace conflicting emotions, and he picked his way past the thorns to accentuate the positive aspects of a spell in which Scotland had climbed almost 40 places in the FIFA rankings:

'I should have been prepared for the goodwill I have encountered through the year, because Craig Brown primed me for it even before I started. He told me I would be amazed by the amount of affection and support there is for the national team across the whole of the country. Craig was right about that, but it was still a terrific surprise to go out and discover the depth and the extent of it. It comes from everywhere, wherever you go, from supporters of all clubs, from the people at the clubs themselves and yes, even from the media. Of course there is a critical side to the press as well, but that is just part of the business. However, this year has definitely shown me that, if you are a bit settled and seem to have something going for you, they are very supportive. I have told our players that, and that they shouldn't allow media criticism to be an excuse for not producing good form. I have also told them that everybody does want us to do well, but it is not something we should be afraid of, something that should put us under pressure. On the contrary it should be embraced and seen as a positive thing, because it is. I knew even before I took the job that Scotland supporters themselves are rather a special group, and I have seen plenty of things to strengthen that opinion. We have been fortunate with them.

'When I look back, my attitude is that not getting to Germany was a disappointment, but it wasn't a massive one. From where we started [two points from the opening three matches] we were going to be dependent on an entire sequence of results involving rivals in matches which were beyond our control. You always hope that things will work in your favour, but from the beginning I had suspected that it wouldn't happen. As long as we were not mathematically out of it though, the hope remained, and that was what made the first half of the home match against Belarus the biggest disappointment of the whole year. We had beaten Norway in Oslo a month earlier, and that day at Hampden everybody was desperate for us to do well, and we didn't. In the first half particularly we just didn't get going, and they seized the goal which eventually won the match.

'All the same I think, unlike 12 months ago, we have now got ourselves into a decent starting position. I don't mean that in terms of the whole squad, of course, but in certain areas of the team. Every new manager's first objective is to sort things out defensively, to make his side difficult to beat, and I think we have made progress in that area, while I've thought from the outset that we were pretty strong in midfield. But it is doing the hardest bit that we still have a bit of work to do. That is taking the initiative and going on to win games. The Belarus experience was a reminder to us all that you don't just have to turn up in order to play well. You have to maintain the progress in the level of performance.

'Whether we can go on to the stage of being able to overcome teams with an attacking game will depend to a great extent on how our younger forwards mature over the coming months. Kenny [Miller] has reacted very well to the pressure of the international game, and James [McFadden] looks as though he has come through a sticky patch at his club [Everton]. Others have to mature and develop. We have given chances – and will continue to do so – to individuals such as Shaun Maloney, Craig Beattie, Derek Riordan, Garry O'Connor and one or two others. They are they key to whether or not we can achieve a more comprehensive game, one in which we can defend solidly, but also create and convert scoring opportunities on a regular basis. And I think that the forward play will be the crux of the matter in determining how well we fare in the forthcoming European Championship qualifying competition, no matter whom we are drawn against.

'But ultimately 2005 has been quite productive. If the goodwill I talked about has been the most pleasant surprise, the most pleasing aspect of the entire exercise so far has been the response we have had from all the players in the squad. During the period we have asked them a variety of questions, and they have tried 100 per cent to come up with the answers. I don't think it is ever possible to say that you are on track or ahead of the game, or that targets have been hit. More accurately it is an ever-evolving process with the primary objective of continuous progress. But from my perspective and that of the other coaches the players could not have offered more, and that is immensely satisfying.'

It was a characteristically sober analysis delivered by a professional who had witnessed almost every foible that football has to offer. If Smith had a complaint with the demands of the Scotland job, it lay in his conviction that these simply were not sufficiently demanding. It was satisfying being responsible for picking up where he had left off with a disparate collection of players only around six or seven times a year, but for the workaholic Glaswegian the national post was a tremendous privilege, and a source of some restlessness. 'Even at 58 I feel the frustration of not having enough to do, of not being involved with the players more, but that just comes with the territory,' he admitted.

If Smith was seeking a major challenge, he could not have asked for a more probing examination than that which emerged from the draw for the 2008 European Championship, which was conducted in Montreux, Switzerland, on 27 January. On that day I was covering a press conference at Heart of Midlothian during a surreal period when the Tynecastle operation seemed to have managers acting as translators and tea-boys running the commercial operation, or vice versa. Reporters had become accustomed to hearing mind-boggling declarations from and being harangued by the Edinburgh club's chairman Vladimir Romanov, but a genuine sense of shock gripped the team's training complex at Heriot-Watt University as the Scots were paired with Italy, France and Ukraine, not to mention Lithuania, Georgia and the Faroe Islands. It was a shark-infested pool, and Scotland would have to knock out one of the sides that had contested the most recent World Cup final to have any chance of reaching the finals of a major tournament for the first time since the 1998 World Cup. Some blanched at the news, but Walter Smith once more impressed European colleagues with a precise summation which confirmed his belief that this was exactly the sort of challenge that could galvanise the Scots to great deeds, considering the manner in which they had traditionally tended to reserve their best displays after they had been written off by the media. There was no self-delusion in this approach: 'Of course it will be hard. France are a wonderful side. So are the Italians. The Ukrainians have been formidable in recent years, and we know that this will be tough for us. But down the years we have relished meeting the best and testing ourselves, and nothing has changed in that respect. We have a few months before the campaign starts, but we have to be positive in our approach. And we will be.'

The obvious media response was to refer to a 'Group of Death' once more and to offer pessimistic forecasts, which rather missed the point that Smith's players were growing in stature. They demonstrated that in resounding fashion by venturing to Japan in May 2006 and winning the Kirin Cup, a tri-nations competition also involving the host country and Bulgaria. In the performance against the eastern Europeans it was possible to detect the blossoming of a new confidence and swagger, Smith having chosen a number of fresh-faced youngsters who responded superbly. Debutants Kris Boyd and Chris Burke produced touches of the sublime in marking up two goals apiece, McFadden joined them in the demolition job, and Scotland recorded a 5-1 victory which was better than any observer could have predicted. The Japanese proved a stiffer proposition and occasionally left Smith's men struggling in defence, but a goalless draw was sufficient for Scotland to lift the silverware, and though it hardly compensated for not being at the World Cup finals, the momentum was building.

That was evident from the clamour for tickets for the opening match of the European qualifiers against the Faroese, opponents from the far north who had sparked embarrassment for Scotland under Berti Vogts when they scored twice in the opening quarter-of-an-hour and were denied victory only thanks to a late rally from the likes of Barry Ferguson, the Scots scraping a 2-2 draw. Smith's squad were in no mood for a repeat, and sent out a ringing declaration of intent with a 6-0 win at Celtic Park, which was as convincing as the result suggests. Boyd led the charge with two goals and Miller, Fletcher, O'Connor and McFadden also contributed. Scotland flew to Kaunas to tackle Lithuania the following week, and again demonstrated their increasing confidence and freedom of movement in achieving a 2-1 success with goals from Miller and Christian Dailly. Scotland's 100 per cent record was maintained in a treacherous group, but next up were France, who had dismantled Scotland frequently in the past and who arrived as runners-up from the World Cup final in Germany. It was an occasion in which logic would have to be ignored for Smith's men to prevail, and yet a strange feeling was abroad in Glasgow on the morning of the game. Foot soldiers from the Tartan Army at Queen Street Station were not merely confident; they had placed wagers on a home win, which seemed somewhat rash. 'You see the French are a bunch of fancy dans. They want to walk the ba' into the net, and we will be in their faces from the kick-off, so I think we'll piss them off so much they'll lose the plot,' ventured Michael from Stonehaven. Alastair from Broughty Ferry maintained to me that Walter Smith would prove the key difference. 'Their manager [Raymond] Domenech is a bit of a flake, and he is also fu' of himself. He will tell his boys it is going to be a walk in the park, and if they go out with that approach, they will find themselves hitting a big brick wall.' Chris from Falkirk said simply: 'They couldnae score at the World Cup. They want it all on their own terms. If we mess with their heads, then we can beat them.'

Scotland's starting XI were Gordon (Hearts), Dailly (West

Ham), Caldwell (Celtic), Pressley (Hearts), Weir (Everton), Alexander (Preston), Hartley (Hearts), Fletcher (Manchester United), Ferguson (Rangers), McCulloch (Wigan) and McFadden (Everton). Domenech called upon some glittering personnel in Coupet (Lyon), Sagnol (Bayern Munich), Thuram (Barcelona), Boumsong (Juventus), Abidal (Lyon), Ribery (Marseille), Vieira (Internazionale), Makelele (Chelsea), Malouda (Lyon), Trezeguet (Juventus) and Henry (Arsenal). For all their recent improvement, Scotland still had to beat a team of significant pedigree under Smith, while France journeyed to the stadium with innate confidence springing from their record of losing just once in 49 previous qualifying games. The optimism expressed by that Tartan Army triumvirate was certainly contagious, and anticipation arose of a performance from the hosts which would shake the French, and the stage was set for one of the great afternoons in Scottish sport.

Smith expected his team to be under siege at the outset, and his concern was justified. The visitors pressed forward with the fluency and flourish expected from talents such as Thierry Henry and Claude Makelele, and they could easily have been a couple of goals in front within 20 minutes, but efforts by Patrick Vieira and David Trezeguet were denied because of offside. The Scots initially struggled to stem the flow, but Smith's unsung heroes gradually repelled their adversaries in stirring fashion . . . and began orchestrating little forays of their own. Hartley launched a series of darting runs which irked then worried the French, and Graham Alexander belied his first division status with a fine display. At the back Gary Caldwell was obdurate, Pressley covered most of the blades of grass on the pitch in harassing and hounding, and Craig Gordon was typically solid as the last line of defence.

The Scots did lose the opening half on points, but Domenech wore a slightly worried expression at the interval. Smith was in his element, praising his men for their discipline and professionalism, and reminding them that they could play a bit themselves. The watchwords were vigilance and precision, for the manager recognised only too well that if France conjured up one goal, they might finish with three or four, so there would be no cavalry charges upfield. On the other hand, if McFadden or McCulloch could carve out one chance, they had to do their damnedest to ensure that it was not squandered. Because, as the Tartan Army chap had suggested, France were one of those teams who could be breathtaking in full spate, but who often struggled to make supremacy tell when it really counted. That thought increasingly inspired Scotland, and suddenly they were on the march, the influential midfield pairing of Fletcher and Ferguson stamping their authority on an increasingly cantankerous Vieira, Makelele and Florent Malouda, as the more discerning supporters cranked up the tempo and the decibel level in recognition of the inspirational exploits which had started to trouble the French resistance. The question on everybody's lips was whether this would bring a breakthrough for Scotland, and in the 67th minute the prayers of a nation were answered when a corner from Hartley swung dangerously into the French 18-yard box, and Caldwell bustled past Eric Abidal to get his foot to the ball and power it into the net. For a few seconds it seemed as though the action had been frozen with supporters en masse checking out whether an offside flag was flapping in the air, but no. It was a priceless goal for Caldwell and his country, and across the land whoops of delight reflected the fact that nothing binds Scotland together more closely than victory against the odds. As I set out to meet friends that night, I recall that everyone seemed to be smiling and that a wee jink had been added to the step of the nation. Constant re-screenings of Caldwell's goal were allied to praise for Walter Smith, who had been close to tears as the fans applauded him. He summed up the action and the outcome:

'It's a tremendous result, and certainly the best I have ever had as a manager. We were under tremendous pressure in the first half and they had one or two chances, but we got stuck in, defended stoutly and benefited from a bit of luck. We want to remain competitive throughout the qualifying campaign, and this is a great start with nine points from three matches. We knew that France would have a lot of possession, and territorially they had us pinned back for a while. But in the second half we improved our passing, and they didn't create many clear chances after that. It is a fantastic win, and a great reward for all the hard work that every single player put into the game.'

Scottish football commanded front-page banner headlines for the right reasons, and though there came a hangover a few days later in Kiev when Ukraine comfortably defeated the team by 2-0, the French triumph embodied most of the prime qualities which the manager had displayed in the service of club or country for the best part of 25 years. Sports journalist Brian Viner wrote in *The Independent*: 'Waiting for Walter Smith in the lounge of the Holiday Inn at Glasgow International Airport, I reflect that if Scotland had won in Ukraine earlier this month, having just dispatched France at Hampden Park to top Euro 2008's killer qualifying Group B, then I might be waiting in the Walter Smith Lounge at the Holiday Inn, or maybe in the lounge at the Walter Smith Holiday Inn, or even in the lounge of the Holiday Inn at Walter Smith International Airport. "Aye, we do tend to go a bit over the top when we win," said Smith, with a smile.' Well, why not? Victories of this magnitude happen infrequently enough for the majority of Scottish people to be uncertain how best to respond. But then Scots with only a marginal interest in football were sufficiently roused by the unexpected defeat of France, and Smith received the accolade of Scot of the Year at the Glenfiddich Spirit of Scotland Awards in December. It was fitting recognition for his success in transforming a bunch of disillusioned young men into a potent fighting unit with the capacity to beat one of the best countries in the world. For a while, at least, he made Scots feel better about themselves and more optimistic about the future. Football may have problems, but it can be an inspirational pursuit, and Smith acknowledged as much when he accepted his prize to a standing ovation and bearing a rather sheepish grin. He promised that he would try to keep up the good work, but further drama was about to unfold.

CHAPTER FIFTEEN

BACK TO IBROX

❖

'He will get the lads playing for the jersey again'

Walter Smith's first love in football was Rangers. Once that passion was ignited as a schoolboy, he cherished the club with his heart and his soul. When he departed Ibrox Stadium in 1998, it was with the sinking feeling that in sport as in life you can never go back. Yet even when he and the redoubtable Archie Knox were ensconced at Everton for three-and-a-half years, the first thing they listened out for every Saturday evening was how Rangers had fared. It should not have been regarded as a surprise then that when the Ibrox club stumbled into difficulties in 2006 and Smith was eventually offered a second chance to assume the manager's role, he weighed up the pros and cons, reflected on what his departure would mean for the Scottish Football Association, and reached his decision within a few minutes. To some, Smith's behaviour in returning to his roots at the beginning of 2007 was an act of betrayal, and the SFA confirmed their intention to take legal action against him, claiming breach of contract, and against Rangers for alleged inducement to breach the contract. David Taylor, the outgoing chief executive of the governing body, summed up the widespread mood beyond the vicinity of Ibrox: 'Walter's departure is a serious blow to the SFA. He has done an excellent job for us and the Scottish national team. We are very disappointed that he has chosen to leave us at this critical time in our Euro 2008 qualification campaign.' In a statement issued on 10 January the SFA added: 'At a meeting this morning with the CEO of the association, Walter Smith delivered a letter of resignation with immediate effect from his position as national coach of the Scotland team. No agreement has been reached with Mr Smith or Rangers Football Club on any compensation payment to be made for the early termination of his employment, which is in breach of contract with the SFA.'

The verbiage obscured the reality that Smith had already signed a three-year deal at Rangers, which would offer him security for the rest of his life. Paying heed to some comments in the Scottish press and on football phone-in programmes, one could have been forgiven for imagining that he was guilty of selling his birthright and his country down the river. The explanation was more prosaic, and embodied Smith's sense of priorities. He had taken the Scotland job while he was unemployed, he had succeeded in resuscitating the moribund patient, and now he was being presented with a fresh challenge by the organisation that he had always supported, and he would be rejoining David Murray, a man he admired enormously. Why all the fuss, hate mail and slanders? I believe that Smith had no reason to apologise for renewing his links with Rangers. He had watched from the sidelines as the sophisticated Frenchman Paul le Guen was wheeled out as Alex McLeish's successor to a fanfare of trumpets and a rapturous reception in the media. But almost as quickly as his star was in the ascendancy, Le Guen's stock plummeted in a flurry of poor transfer signings and miserable results allied to his failure to command the respect of key players and his deficiencies in adapting to the demands of the Scottish game. It was not as if Smith had wakened suddenly and thought: 'I'm scooting off to Rangers.' He had highlighted his frustration at not having access to his international players except on a sporadic basis, and his pronouncements during the previous autumn, when he spoke openly about his desire to get involved with club football again, could hardly have carried a clearer message that he was not prepared to commit himself indefinitely to the Scotland post. Smith at 58 knew the clock was ticking, that he could not afford to hang around in what he regarded as part-time employment, and that he would be obliged to stay with Scotland whether or not they qualified for the finals of the leading competitions. That held no appeal, hence his itchy feet.

As for those Celtic followers who have alleged that Smith took the Scotland job to get back into practice for Rangers, I would simply ask: are they seriously arguing that he deduced that Le Guen would prove to be a flop over a year before he was appointed? Is it not more probable that if the French coach had lived up to his star billing and steered the Ibrox team towards the Champions League, that Smith would have found another club in the English Premiership or the SPL? He had declared to *The Herald* in November 2006:

'To return to club football it would have to be the right job, and I would need to be able to do what I wanted to do. Everybody is competitive, and I suppose that I feel I would like to redress the situation [in England] and have another crack at it down there if the circumstances were right. When I left Everton, I considered myself a failure. I wanted to make them a stable, top-six side like they were in the 1980s, but I was there at the wrong time, and I never left anything for David Moyes except a young Wayne Rooney, and even then that had nothing to do with me, so David had done a better job at Goodison than I managed. But yes, returning to club management is something that has occurred to me, and I haven't ruled it out.'

These are not the words of a man who was waiting patiently to fill Le Guen's boots as soon as he had exited Ibrox under a cloud. Instead they serve to indicate that Smith was pleased to be able to assist his country in extricating themselves from the mire, but he did not consider it a long-term career option. This makes perfect sense for those acquainted with Smith's relish for training-ground banter, the daily exchange of news, gossip and jokes which are the lifeblood of any club, and which were denied him when he was meeting up with his Scotland squad five or six times a year.

No sooner had Smith arrived at Ibrox again than he was orchestrating another revival. The title race had long since been settled through a combination of Celtic's early-season supremacy and Le Guen's errors, but Murray assured his old friend that there would be money to spend in the summer, and the priority was for Smith to ensure that his team qualified for the Champions League. It was as if the rewind button had been set for a decade before. There was the manager marshalling his troops with the sturdy invective which had not changed throughout his career; and alongside was Ally McCoist, a coiled spring of energy, grins and remarks. The message from both was straightforward: Rangers had under-performed this season, their results had not been good enough for a club of their reputation, and some players needed to take a hard look at themselves in the mirror and ask whether they deserved to remain at Ibrox. No-nonsense stuff. Though Smith knew from his first inspection of the Rangers squad that serious treatment would be required come the summer, he had immediate business to hand. On Saturday, 13 January he returned to what seemed like his natural dwelling-place, the technical area at Ibrox. He reinstated as captain Barry Ferguson, a player he admired and trusted to bring the side together. The Scotland player responded with a brilliant display capped by a goal in 88 minutes, as Rangers transcended awful weather to power to the kind of overwhelming victory which had eluded them under Le Guen. The home side subjected Dundee United to a 5-0 flogging, goals from Charlie Adam and Chris Burke and two from Kris Boyd preceding the Ferguson strike. This Rangers player has his critics, on both sides of the Old Firm, but here he was wonderful in full flow, and he directed the action as if orchestrating the tempo of the match. Round about him the young Scots Adam, Burke, Boyd and Murray were hives of industry, and while there were still occasional signs of the defensive vulnerability which had blighted the Ibrox men throughout the season, their midfield was a sight to behold. Several of the men in blue recognised they were fighting for their futures, but on a bog-like pitch whose state had persuaded referee Craig Mackay to consider abandoning the match at the interval, there was no denying the efficacy or pace of the Rangers showing.

As *Scotland on Sunday* saw it: 'This was more like it. This was a world away from what we have seen from them this season. Throughout the Rangers ranks there was industry and urgency, there was a desire to play at a tempo several notches higher than before, and a ruthlessness in front of goal that brought them, by far and away, their most thumping victory of the season.' Smith expressed pleasure at his side's performance, but declined to take any of the credit. Even in these early days he had twigged that Le Guen had recruited several players, including Karl Svensson and Jeremy Clement, who were not equipped for the hurly-burly of the SPL, and that he would have to strengthen his defence when he could. But the screams of delight from the Rangers faithful, who had been fed a diet of dross for so long, was music to the ears, and in the directors' box David Murray must have allowed himself a significant sigh of relief. And as Rangers grew increasingly impressive, it became clear that Paul Gascoigne had been correct in his analysis that Smith would be capable of implementing a swift turnaround in the team's fortunes. The controversial former player had opined:

'Walter knows how to get the best out of all different types of people, and mark my words, he knows what is required to get in front of Celtic, and it will be his aim to finish second in the league this season and then win it next year. He will get the lads playing for the jersey again, and will sign players who deserve to be at Ibrox. In recent years not enough players have actually deserved the honour of pulling on the Rangers jersey, but I am sure that will all change from now on. Walter will also bring fear and a winning mentality to the dressing room. Before games he demanded a 3-0 lead at half-time, and during the break he would want to see us win 6-0 by the finish. And he was as hard on himself as he was on his players, if he thought that he had made a mistake. So I have no doubts whatsoever that his return is terrific news for Rangers.'

In domestic terms the recovery was well under way, but there remained the tricky problem of transplanting impressive form to European competition, and Smith must have felt a twinge of *déjà vu* when he attempted to negotiate his side past Spanish opponents Osasuna in the last 16 of the UEFA Cup in March. In recent SPL encounters at Ibrox the Scottish team had been indomitable and created numerous opportunities in most matches, yet they seemed to suffer from stage fright against Osasuna, and were lucky to record a 1-1 draw in the first leg. Smith described it as the worst display since his return to the club. That underwhelming showing left his squad with a difficult away match, and once again they toiled on their travels. Bernardo Romeo and Gomez Juanlo squandered excellent chances in the first half as Rangers were confronted with sustained pressure. Despite Charlie Adam and Gavin Rae coming close for the visitors, there was a sense of inevitability when Pierre Webo scored in the 71st minute to send Osasuna through to the quarter-finals of the event. It was frustrating enough that Smith's side had not done themselves justice, but worse that there was a disquieting recurrence of a traditional problem from their followers. 'We hoped to play a little better tonight than we did, especially in the first half, but it was not to be,' said the manager. 'At the end of the day we simply did not create enough opportunities. We played reasonably well in some aspects, but overall we weren't up to scratch, and I was particularly disappointed with how we performed in Glasgow.'

If these words sounded familiar, so did some sectarian chants which echoed from the stands as a small but vocal number of so-called fans disgraced themselves and heaped trouble on Rangers in the process. UEFA fined the club £8,000 after 'improper conduct' by their fans during the Osasuna tie, but the rather sickened expressions of Smith and Martin Bain, the Rangers chief executive, spoke volumes for their vexation at how this issue kept arising and threatened increasingly stiff punishments for the club, including the possibility of being banned from Europe in the future. Thus they had barely returned from Spain when they launched a new campaign, Follow with Pride, in a bid finally to nail the blight of bigotry. 'Everyone at Ibrox is committed to showing Rangers in the best possible light on and off the field, and that is why we are launching this initiative,' said Ally McCoist, who once expressed his mystification to me that so many supporters could roar on Rangers teams containing Catholic players such as Lorenzo Amoruso and Rino Gattuso, and yet still resort to shouting 'F*** the Pope' at opponents. 'Follow with Pride is all about promoting sporting behaviour among fans and the great work that the club does in bringing together all types of people in the community. The club is constantly under the spotlight, and our fans more than anybody else realise the importance of setting high standards of behaviour. So for the good of everybody, we have to get that message across and show what a fantastic club this is, not for some, but for all.'

The sentiments were admirable, but one suspects that this fundamental malaise will not be solved in the near future, particularly with the prospect that the Old Firm will again dominate the SPL in coming seasons. Smith has proved that he is a master in the art of beating his club's biggest rivals, and it was no surprise that he should continue his successful sequence, courtesy of Ugo Ehiogu's rather surreal winning goal which silenced the majority of the capacity crowd at Celtic Park on 11 March and subsequently when Rangers encountered Celtic at Ibrox on 5 May. In fairness to the visitors, they had gone off the boil with their emphatic championship win all but wrapped up, but that should not detract from the supremacy which the hosts displayed throughout their 2-0 triumph, a result that could have been significantly better but for missed chances and last-gasp defending. 'I thought we started well, and I felt that we fully deserved our victory,' said Smith, reflecting on the goals from Boyd and Adam which had earned the three points. 'The main objective was to clinch the Champions League qualifying spot, but a lot of the boys have found a good level of consistency, and that is very heartening. We kept good possession, we maintained our discipline, and my squad have shown a terrific attitude since I arrived back here. We haven't lost a league game since that time, but we know that both ourselves and Celtic will improve next season, so the work never stops. In fact, I reckon that it will be a very, very busy summer.'

Walter Smith more than anyone recognises the problems that lie ahead for him and for Rangers. Close friend David Murray has spent nearly 20 years on the bridge, and he made clear at the most recent annual general meeting that he was prepared to sell the club 'to the right person'. In future there will not be £12m available to buy such as Tore Andre Flo, and Smith will be required to display every ounce of guile that he possesses to win back the SPL title. Yet it would be difficult to find anybody better equipped to handle that challenge. His grasp of statistics and the details of transfer dealing is illuminating:

'It's not any different from the last time when I was at Rangers. People say that it is, but that's a bit of a fallacy. We couldn't outbid most clubs in the 1990s. During my first three years at Ibrox we operated at a profit in the transfer market, and that was because we were fortunate enough to get £6m for Trevor Steven. Paul Gascoigne cost us £3.4m, but at that time that was just the market value. A lot of really good players were going for that kind of money, and it is just how the market goes. If you go for a number of players and make offers, it will not happen that you will have them all accepted. You always get to the stage where you have a figure you would pay for the player, and sometimes it takes a while before the to-ing and fro-ing reaches that level. No club ever gets all the players on their list. It doesn't happen. You hear about clubs with more financial clout than us getting beaten by clubs with even more financial clout. Quite a lot of clubs don't even start until September. Then there are the awkward bits, and it can be a wee bit frustrating. You know the sensible view to take is that it might not all come together.'

Irrespective of these considerations, Smith's forays into the transfer market in the summer of 2007 appeared to be shrewd investments. There may have been initial reservations over the fitness of Bosman signing Jean-Claude Darcheville, but he started terrorising defences, while Daniel Cousin, Carlos Cuellar and DaMarcus Beasley impressed as Rangers demonstrated that they would present a much sterner test for Celtic in the 2007-08 campaign. I have few doubts that if it boils down to a psychological battle between Walter Smith and Gordon Strachan, there will be only one winner. And it won't be the diminutive manager from Edinburgh. But that is for the future. In 2008 Smith will turn 60, yet on the evidence of his wheeling and dealing in the transfer market and his training-ground joshing with Ally McCoist, he is still basking in his natural habitat: moulding, developing and grooming players in the grand Ibrox tradition, and hunting restlessly for European honours. No matter that the latter task has proved tough in the extreme for the men of Ibrox, the place where he and his grandfather thrilled to the sight of blue-clad warriors giving their all for what they believed was the greatest club in the world.

And, as Walter Smith will tell you, Rangers remain just that.

INDEX

❖